Learn
Table Tennis
in a Weekend

LEARN TABLE TENNIS IN A WEEKEND

ANDRZEJ GRUBBA

Photography by Hanna and Maciej Musiał

DORLING KINDERSLEY
London • New York • Sydney • Moscow

A DORLING KINDERSLEY BOOK

Editor Ian Wisniewski
DTP Designer Sonia Charbonnier
Managing Editor Francis Ritter
Managing Art Editor Derek Coombes
Production Controller Patricia Harrington

Consultant Adam Giersz
Editor Dariusz Kozłowski
Proofreader Bożena Leszkowicz
Translator Magda Hannay
Graphic Design: STUDIO PP - Paweł Pasternak, Grzegorz Dworak
Pre-press: STUDIO PP - Paweł Pasternak

2 4 6 8 10 9 7 5 3 1

First published in Poland in 1996
by Wydawnictwo Wiedza i Życie S.A., Warsaw

A CIP catalogue record for this book
is available from the British Library

ISBN 0 7513 0483 2

Printed and bound in Singapore by KHL Printing Co Pte Ltd.

CONTENTS

·

Introduction 6

PREPARING FOR THE WEEKEND 8

Equipment......................10
At the table....................16
Shaping up 18

The grip.........................22
The ready position 24
Types of stroke and spin.....26

THE WEEKEND COURSE 28

Day 1

Bat and ball exercises.......30
Backhand 32
Forehand 36

Service 42
Service return.................48

Day 2

Forehand drive 50
Backhand drive 54
Blocking topspin balls.......58
The winning smash.........60
Defensive lobbing...........64

Elements of
defensive play.................68
Developing tactics
and match play...............72

AFTER THE WEEKEND 74

Rules and regulations 76
Doubles 78
Tactics in singles matches...82

Shots for advanced players...84
Final comments 88

Glossary 92
Index 94

INTRODUCTION

DID YOU KNOW THAT TABLE TENNIS is played by so many people that it ranks alongside soccer as the world's most popular sport? The popularity of table tennis reflects its exciting nature and health benefits. It requires relatively inexpensive equipment, there is effectively no age limit for players, and it is possible to learn the basics of the game in a weekend, although mastering the game requires time and effort. During my 25 years of competitive play, I have come to know the game intimately. In this book I want to introduce the elements of the game, using simple and clear instructions, making it easy for you to understand the secrets of various strokes. An essential element of learning is the ability to visualize every movement that is described. Therefore, you should not limit yourself solely to learning how to hit the ball. Think of ways to improve your game, even while away from the table. Discuss your play with your coach or someone who

watches you from the sidelines. With experience, you will realize that individual elements of the game do not have to be identical for every player. In fact, a great attraction of table tennis is that your playing technique not only reflects your own personality, but also helps you to develop skills such as the ability to cope under pressure. A green table and a small celluloid ball can be the beginning of a great table tennis adventure, which should not be limited to weekends. I hope this will be so in your case.

Good luck!

ANDRZEJ GRUBBA

PREPARING FOR THE WEEKEND

The right preparation will ensure that learning is effective and enjoyable

TRY TO FIND A FREE WEEKEND that you can devote to learning the game of table tennis, using a room where you will be able to concentrate fully on the series of exercises detailed in this book. Ideally, you should start a fitness programme a few weeks in advance of the weekend. Your bat should initially be inexpensive, not too heavy, and with a thin layer of rubber covering both sides of the plywood. If you cannot find a partner to train with, you can always use a ball-throwing device. While a single ball is sufficient to play the game, you should have between 30-40 balls to make training with a partner more effective, or about 100 balls when playing

BATS
Learn about different bat designs, which are suited to the different playing styles (see p.10).

BALLS
Before buying the balls, check which ones should be used for practice and which for playing matches (see p.12).

CLOTHING
Suitable clothing, the correct equipment, and a suitable partner will make the learning process more enjoyable (see p.14).

with a ball-throwing machine. Wear suitable shoes and clothing that will not restrict your movement (shorts, a short-sleeved shirt, and perhaps a track suit). Your socks should be made of cotton or wool, and you will also need a towel. Meanwhile, start to learn the basics of the game, including grips, the starting position, and various strokes.

SHOES
Soft rubber soles will prevent sore feet and blisters (see p.15).

GRIP
Learn the two basic ways of holding the bat – the European (**shake-hands**) grip and the Asian (**penholder**) grip (see pp.22-23).

TABLE
Check the size and design of the table (see p.16).

FITNESS
Physical fitness and supple muscles will help you to learn table tennis more quickly (see pp.18-21).

EQUIPMENT

Choosing the bat, balls, clothing, and footwear

ONE OF THE MOST IMPORTANT DECISIONS to make is the choice of type of bat. The design of its principal components, which are the **blade** and the surface, actually determines the type of game that will be played. Beginners tend to choose a bat with fixed (as opposed to replaceable) rubber surfaces. The sides are usually identical, although some bats offer a smooth (reversed) and a pimpled surface.

THE BAT

When choosing a bat it is important to remember that:
- it should not be too heavy
- it should have a comfortable grip
- its rubber surfaces should offer a moderate grip and speed, which means a thickness of not more than 1.5mm.

A bat with these characteristics will be suitable for beginners, as well as being an inexpensive purchase. However, should you decide to buy a more expensive bat, it is important to enquire about the characteristics of the blade and the rubber surfaces.

BLADES

Blades vary, depending on the shape of the bat's head and handle. Typical handles are straight, anatomic, or flared. Blades vary according to the:
- layers of plywood (5-7),
- weight 70-90g (2.5-3oz),
- speed and control.

Blades are also graded as:
- **fast** – with limited

control for aggressive match play;
- **slow** – with greater control for defensive play;
- **all-round** – for any type of game.

To comply with ITTF regulations, blades must comprise 85 per cent natural wood. The other 15 per cent can include materials such as carbon fibre.

RUBBER SURFACES

• **Dimpled-surface** – this version is composed of two layers, including a spongy base and a rubber overlay featuring dimples. The result is a highly flexible base and a surface with a good grip. The thickness of the surface layers should exceed 2mm for aggressive and spin play. For all-round play, it should be 1.7-2.0mm, and for a defensive game it should be less than 1.7mm.

• **Pimpled-surface** – this comprises two layers with outward-facing pimples that provide greater speed and spin. It is also less sensitive to an opponent's spin than the reversed style. Many world-class players favour a combination of a pimpled surface (usually on the backhand side of the bat) and a dimpled surface (on the forehand side).

• **Special rubber surface** – this is generally used for defensive play. The surface includes rubber with long pimples and so-called "anti-topspins". When coming into contact with the ball, the long, thin pimples absorb the impact and also bend to give the ball spin. The anti-topspin rubber surfaces have pimples that face inwards, which ensures a very low level of friction.

Colours of rubber surfaces are dictated by the ITTF (International Table Tennis Federation) – one side must be red, the other black, while the maximum thickness of rubber allowed is 4mm.

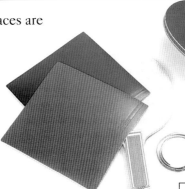

SPONGY RUBBERS
When buying rubber surfaces, check if they are properly sealed in a cellophane wrapper: rubber that has been exposed to the air loses its grip.

THE CATAPULT EFFECT

The development of sponge-backed rubber, and its introduction into the game in the 1950s, has revolutionized table tennis. The flexibility and elasticity of this type of rubber, combined with the increased grip provided by the outer layer, significantly increase the speed and spin of the ball. In return, this makes match play far more exciting.

BALLS

Table tennis balls are produced either from celluloid or plastic. Each ball is stamped with a motif that indicates the level of quality. The finest balls feature either three stars or a registered mark of approval for use in official matches, which is granted by the National or World Table Tennis Federation. A ball weighs 2.5g and is 38mm in diameter. Balls are usually sold in packets of 3, 6, or 12. The colour of the ball, which may be opaque white or an opaque yellow-orange, should be appropriate to the colour of the table. The yellow-orange balls are generally used on blue tables, and white balls on green tables.

Do not buy balls that have not been stamped, are out of shape, or have a visible groove along the join. This indicates a ball of poor quality and will detract from your enjoyment of the game.

BAT COVERS

Depending on the type, a bat cover may hold one or two bats. Stiff covers, which have been reinforced with wood or plastic, are recommended to protect the bats against accidental damage. Some covers also include pockets in which to carry balls.

• **SPRAY**
For removing dirt and grease from the rubber surface.

ADDITIONAL EQUIPMENT

• **RUBBER ADHESIVE**
Experienced players change the rubber surfaces of their bats regularly, often reusing surfaces that have already seen service. Fresh adhesive increases the flexibility and elasticity of rubber.

• **BRUSH**
Used to clean pimpled rubber surfaces.

• **SPONGE**
Used to wash dimpled rubber surfaces and, when dampened, it removes surface dirt.

• **EDGING TAPE**
Prevents separation of the rubber surfaces and protects the edges of the blade against damage.

• **HANDLE TAPE**
Usually a piece of soft leather, wound around the handle to absorb sweat during play.

CLOTHING

Clothing should be comfortable
and not restrict movement.
It should also be made from
light, easily washable fabrics,
in colours that contrast with
that of the ball.

SHIRT •
Short-sleeved,
preferably cotton,
and typically
open-necked.

SHORTS •
Loosely fitting, made
of light, airy fabric, and
matching the colour of
the shirt.

SOCKS •
Thick, preferably
cotton, which
absorbs perspiration.

SHOES •
Comfortable shoes
enable quick
movements
around the table.

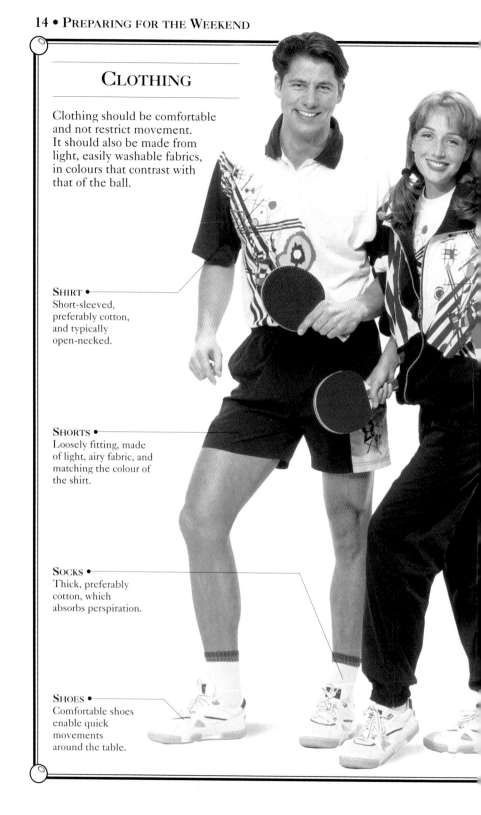

FOOTWEAR

The most appropriate type of footwear for table tennis has a low heel and a ridged rubber sole, and should be strong enough to suit the type of floor surface that is being played on. The most important part of the shoe is an orthopaedic insert. This protects the heel against impact with the floor, while also minimizing and absorbing other stresses and strains that act on the foot.

TRACK SUIT

This is an important item of clothing that should be worn during warm-up exercises, and also during breaks in order to prevent excessive heat loss.

SOCKS

Changing into a fresh pair of sports socks during a break can make your game more comfortable.

TENNIS BAG

This should be large enough to contain everything needed for the game, and also for maintaining personal hygiene after playing.

AT THE TABLE

Before you start learning to play, familiarize yourself with the setting

TABLE TENNIS TABLES HAVE BEEN PRODUCED for more than 80 years.
The standard table is 274cm (9ft) long, 152.5cm (5ft) wide, and
76cm (2½ft) high. The net is secured at the edges, and runs across the
middle of the table, being stretched to stand 15.25cm (6in) above
the playing surface. The edges of the table are marked with a white
line that is 2cm (¾in) wide. A continuous white line, 3mm (⅛in)
thick, divides the table into two halves, and marks the service areas
for doubles. The wide variety of materials that can be used in the
manufacturing process means that tables may differ considerably in
their technical characteristics (in terms of friction, elasticity, and
rigidity). The colour of the playing surface is regulated by the
ITTF and must be dark matt in various shades of green or blue.

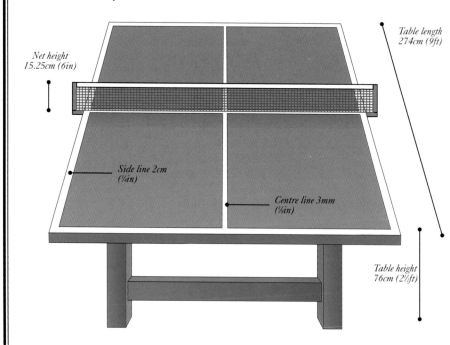

Table length
274cm (9ft)

Net height
15.25cm (6in)

Side line 2cm
(¾in)

Centre line 3mm
(⅛in)

Table height
76cm (2½ft)

Width of the doubles service area 76.25cm (2½ft)

Table width 152.5cm (5ft)

The rules of the game are strictly determined by the ITTF:
- the overall playing area, for one table, must be at least 14m (about 46ft) long, 7m (about 23ft) wide, and 4m (about 13ft) high;
- the minimum strength of light at every point must not fall below 1000 lux;
- the floor must not be made of concrete, brick, or stone, and it must be flat over the entire playing area;
- the surrounding area must be of a dark colour.

TYPES OF TABLES

In order to gain the approval of national or international federations, the playing surface of the table must be such that a ball dropped vertically onto it from a height of 30cm (1ft) bounces back to a height of at least 23cm (about 9in).

The type of bounce that the table provides is determined not only by the choice of material used for the playing surface (chipboard or plywood), but also by the type of legs (wood or metal), as well as the quality and thickness of the varnish on the playing surface.

The so-called **rollaway** tables (on castors) are becoming increasingly popular. They are easy to move around, and, because they can also be folded, they require far less storage space.

BALL-THROWING MACHINE

This type of equipment is now frequently used for training. By varying the type of spin, direction, speed, and frequency of the ball, these machines successfully imitate the conditions of actual match play.

SHAPING UP

The following exercises will help you to improve mobility

BEFORE YOU START PRACTISING with a bat, try to improve your fitness level. General physical fitness, which includes strength, speed, and agility, can be improved through regular exercise. Speed and co-ordination are particularly important for table tennis, and suitable exercises involve the muscles of the lower leg, foot, and joints. Most of the following exercises are aimed at improving the muscle groups that determine how quickly you can react to your opponent's shots. These exercises will also help you to avoid injuries during practice and match play.

SQUATS
Stand with your legs apart and your arms stretched forwards; raise yourself up on your toes and lower your body into a squatting position, keeping your back straight. Repeat 15 times.

SKIPPING
This simple exercise should be performed looking straight ahead and keeping your back straight; jump on your toes, using one or both legs. Try to do as many repetitions as you can within 30 seconds.

SEMI PRESS-UPS
Stand about 1m (3ft) from the table, then lean forwards to hold the edge of the table with both hands. Push away forcefully, and then return to your original standing position, keeping your back straight at all times.

SPEED TRAINING

- Take large steps to the right, over 3-4m (about 10-13ft), then step back to your original position, moving as quickly as you can. Repeat the exercise for 20 seconds.
- Using a running action, move forward over a distance of 3-4m (about 10-13ft), before "running" backwards to your original position. Repeat the exercise for 20 seconds.
- Run as fast as you can along the width of the table, sliding your left/right hand along the edge of the table as you run back and forth. Repeat the exercise for 20 seconds.
- Run back and forth several times over a distance of 15m (about 50ft), within a set time limit; keep increasing your speed within the same time limit, and take a 1-minute break after each session.

BACK STRETCH

Lie on your stomach with your toes outstretched and your arms pointing forwards, slightly bent at the elbow. Gently lift your arms and legs off the ground, simultaneously, before lowering them again. Repeat 30 times.

SCISSORS

Lying on your back, lift both legs slightly above the ground and stretch out your toes. Then move your legs up and down in a "scissor" motion, for about 20 seconds. Take a short break and repeat the exercise, moving your legs horizontally.

STEP-UPS

Place your body weight onto your right foot, then place the left foot onto a step 30cm (1ft) high. Keep your back straight and your arms bent at the elbows. Step up and down rhythmically, ideally on your toes, for about 20 seconds, then repeat the exercise leading with your right foot.

A simple and effective way of improving your stamina is middle and long-distance running up to 1000m (1010yds) and 4km (2½ miles) respectively. Gradually increase your running distance and speed. This form of exercise improves the oxygen supply within the body, while also improving circulation.

STRETCHING EXERCISES

To help realize your potential, and to be fully prepared for matchplay, you need to develop agility as well as building your muscles. Fit muscles are essential for good co-ordination, and this is one of the most important elements of playing table tennis. Maintain your usual breathing rate while carrying out these exercises, which should be performed carefully in order to avoid any possibility of injury.

STOMACH STRETCH

Start from a standing position in front of a wall, then bend backwards and stretch your arms behind you to rest the palms on the wall. Maintain this position for 20 seconds.

THIGH STRETCH

Sit on the floor with your legs and arms stretched forwards and the fingers interlocked. Keeping your back straight, push your body forwards. Hold for about 15 seconds.

SHOULDER STRETCH

With one arm bent across your chest, use your other hand to push the elbow as far as possible towards the opposite shoulder. Repeat for 15 seconds.

ARM AND BACK STRETCH

Place one hand on the opposite shoulder, and use the other hand to push the elbow backwards and downwards. Repeat for 15 seconds, feeling the stretch in your chest and shoulder muscles.

STRETCHING THE HIP JOINTS

Lean forwards as far as you can, resting your hands on your outstretched knee and keeping your back straight; then push the hips forwards as far as you can. Remain in this position for about 20 seconds.

STRETCHING THE THIGH LIGAMENTS

Stand with your feet as far apart as possible, then push your hips forwards. Remain in this position for 20 seconds.

STRETCHING THE CHEST MUSCLES

Stand with your face approximately 50cm (20in) away from the corner of a room. Rest your outstretched hands against each wall, at shoulder height, and lean forwards. Hold this position for about 20 seconds.

STRETCHING THE CALF MUSCLES

Stand a short distance from a wall, keeping your back straight. Lean forwards, resting your hands against the wall at shoulder height, and keeping your feet squarely on the floor. Remain in this position for about 20 seconds.

THE GRIP

Gripping the bat correctly is essential for mastering a variety of strokes

THERE ARE TWO WAYS TO HOLD a table
tennis bat: the **shake-hands** grip
(favoured by European players) and
the **penhold** grip (mainly used in
Asia). The shake-hands grip is
increasingly popular with players, because it
offers the option of using both sides of the bat,
and consequently of using two different types of
rubber surface (such as the anti-spin type for the
backhand and for aggressive **forehand play**). Because
of the enormous popularity of the shake-hands grip with
beginners, this book devotes more space to the shake-hands
grip than to its Asian equivalent.

THE PENHOLD GRIP

This grip is similar to that used to hold a pen or
a pencil. The ball is hit using only one side of
the bat, which is covered in rubber. The thumb
and the index finger are used to grip the
handle, on the side of the bat that is covered
by rubber. The remaining fingers support the
back of the handle. The other side of the bat
should be painted black or red (depending on
the colour of the rubber surface).

The two different types of
grip also entail two separate
playing styles. The picture on
the right shows Olympic
medallist and World
Champion Kim Taek Soo of
Korea, employing the penhold
grip; on the left is the author,
using the shake-hands grip.

THE SHAKE-HANDS GRIP

The handle is held using the palm of the hand, with the index finger outstretched and always resting on the backhand side of the bat. The position of the thumb indicates the forehand side of the bat. The depth of the grip is a matter of each player's personal preference. However, it should be remembered that the position of the index finger, which acts as an extension of the arm, should allow uninhibited movement, and not restrict the use of the racket face. Try not to alter the grip, whatever type of stroke you are playing. The only exception to this rule is a side grip, when using a forehand serve.

INDEX FINGER
This should rest firmly on the head of the bat, supporting it on the backhand side.

THUMB
Placed on the forehand side, it helps to stabilize the bat within the palm.

THE READY POSITION

The correct stance and position at the table, using the shake-hands grip

In order to master the game of table tennis, you must initially learn how to assume the ready position. This stance, together with knowing where to position yourself at the table, are essential elements of the sport.

THE READY POSITION

This position precedes every move around the table. Similarly, you should return to the ready position as quickly as possible after playing each shot. The bat should remain clearly visible to you at all times.

• EYES
The table should remain within your field of vision at all times.

YOUR PLAYING ARM •
Hold the bat forwards, above the playing surface, and about 1m (3ft) above the floor. By holding the bat in a neutral position, you can play a forehand or backhand equally quickly.

CONCENTRATION
Having assumed the ready position, concentrate fully.

FOOTWORK
Standing with your feet apart, slightly more than the width of your shoulders, will help to stabilize your position.

POSITION AT THE TABLE

The correct position at the table for returning an opponent's service (when starting the game) is different for left- and right-handed players. Assume the ready position, standing about 30cm (1ft) away from the table and holding the bat above the playing surface. A right-handed player should stand near the left-hand corner of the table, between the centre line and the left-hand sideline. Similarly, a left-handed player should stand near the right-hand corner of the table. The correct positions to assume for strokes other than the service return depend on how the rally proceeds.

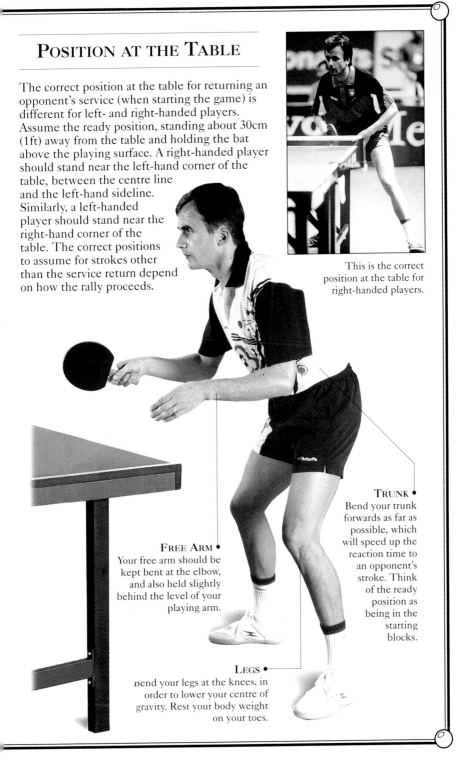

This is the correct position at the table for right-handed players.

TRUNK •
Bend your trunk forwards as far as possible, which will speed up the reaction time to an opponent's stroke. Think of the ready position as being in the starting blocks.

FREE ARM •
Your free arm should be kept bent at the elbow, and also held slightly behind the level of your playing arm.

LEGS •
bend your legs at the knees, in order to lower your centre of gravity. Rest your body weight on your toes.

TYPES OF STROKE AND SPIN

Table tennis revolves around different types of spin, with the type of spin applied depending on the character of the stroke

THE TYPE AND DEGREE OF SPIN applied to the ball depend on various factors. The most important are: a player's position in relation to the ball, the ability to read the type of spin, and the type of bat used. In terms of the range and strength of spins that are possible, table tennis is unequalled among sports, and the ability to read spin correctly is a key difficulty in learning the game.

TYPES OF STROKE

The type of stroke played (as well as the type of spin applied) will determine the ball's direction, trajectory, and the height of the bounce. Even a slight alteration in the angle of the bat in relation to the ball will affect the character of the spin.

• **Topspin** – by holding the bat at an acute angle above the playing surface, the ball is hit using a forward and upward movement, which imparts it with topspin.

• **Chop and push** – by holding the bat at an obtuse angle above the playing surface, the ball is hit using a forward and downward movement, which imparts backspin.

• **Half-volley** – this is played by meeting the oncoming ball with an "open" bat, which returns the ball without imparting any spin.

• **Sidespin** – by holding the bat at a neutral angle and moving the bat parallel to the edge of the table, sidespin – either to the left or the right – is imparted to the ball.

TYPES OF SPIN

• **Topspin** – imparts the ball with a forward spin as it leaves the bat. It is achieved by moving the bat forwards and upwards at the point of contact with the ball.

• **Backspin** – imparts the ball with a backward spin as it leaves the bat. It is achieved by moving the bat in a **chop** (a) and **push** (b) action at the point of · contact with the ball.

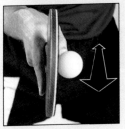

• **Sidespin** – imparts the ball with a spin that curves its trajectory either to the left or right. It is achieved by moving the bat parallel to the edge of the table at the point of contact with the ball.

• **Combination spin** – a combined topspin-sidespin or backspin-sidespin.

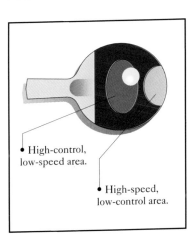

• High-control, low-speed area.

• High-speed, low-control area.

The type of spin applied to the ball is determined at the point of contact with the bat. A comprehensive stroke, which can impart any type of spin to the ball, is the service action. In theory, there is also another option – the "no-spin" ball. However, this is rarely seen in match-play, because it is easy to return. The closest to the no-spin shot that players use is the **half-volley** stroke.

THE WEEKEND COURSE

Making a timetable

THIS COURSE OF TWELVE LESSONS covers eleven essential techniques. DAY ONE entails practising with the bat and learning basic backhand and forehand strokes, the serve, and how to return serve. DAY TWO covers **forehand** and **backhand topspin** shots, and returning topspin shots using a block, smash, or defensive lob. Finally, you will learn the basics of defensive play. If you are unable to master a stroke in the time allocated, don't be discouraged, simply return to it later. After the first day you should have a good feel for the game; after the second day you will be ready for match play.

Spin

DAY 1		Hours	Page
SKILL 1	Bat and ball exercises	1	30-31
SKILL 2	Backhand	1½	32-35
SKILL 3	Forehand	1½	36-41
SKILL 4	Service	1	42-47
SKILL 5	Service return	1	48-49

Learning the forehand

SYMBOLS

THE CLOCK DIAGRAM

All the exercises are accompanied by a diagram of a clock. The blue area on the clock indicates the approximate time that is required to learn the new skill. The grey area on the clock indicates the total time that has been spent on previous lessons.

THE DEGREE OF DIFFICULTY

This is indicated by the number of dots. The easiest exercises to perform feature a single dot •, whereas the most

Right hand

Left hand

difficult exercises have three dots •••. The descriptions of exercises are intended for right-handed players; left-handed players should follow a "mirror image" of these instructions.

DAY 2

		Hours	Page
SKILL 6	Forehand drive	1	50-53
SKILL 7	Backhand drive	1	54-57
SKILL 8	Blocking topspin balls	1	58-59
SKILL 9	The winning smash	1	60-63
SKILL 10	Defensive lobbing	1½	64-67
SKILL 11	Elements of defensive play	1½	68-71
SKILL 12	Developing tactics and match play	1	72-73

Defensive lob

Cross-court forehand

Footwork

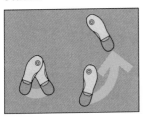

Backhand follow through

1 BAT AND BALL EXERCISES

DAY 1

Start to develop your own instinct for the game, and a natural "feel" for the ball

BOUNCING THE BALL ON A BAT may seem like a simple exercise, but it does develop a degree of ball control. If these exercises pose any problems, adapt them to suit your level of skill.

OBJECTIVE: To assess and improve your ability to judge the direction and speed of the ball. *Rating* from • to ••, depending on your natural co-ordination.

HOLDING THE BAT

Step 1
Starting in the ready position, bounce the ball on your bat by alternating between backhand and forehand strokes. Start by bouncing the ball quite high, then gradually reduce the height. Once you have mastered this, try to bounce the ball by alternating between one side and the edge of the bat.

Step 2
Stand 2-3m (6½-10ft) from a wall. Try to hit the ball so you can return it as the ball bounces off the wall. Initially only play backhands, then alternate between both sides.

Step 3
Stand 3m (10ft) from the wall, and hit the ball so that it returns to you after bouncing off the floor.

Hitting the ball with the edge of the bat may seem difficult at first, but with practice it should not present any difficulties.

BALL EXERCISES

Step 1
Using one hand, throw a ball (it does not have to be a table tennis ball) against a wall, and catch it with the other hand. Do not follow the returning ball with your eyes, but keep it within your field of vision.

Step 2
Stand 5m (16ft) from your partner and throw the ball to each other. Gradually increase the degree of difficulty by varying the speed and type of throw. You can also perform this exercise on your own. Throw the ball against a wall and catch it as the ball returns, first with both hands and then one hand. You can make the exercise more difficult by using a second ball. Building up speed, try various ways of passing the ball to your partner, such as bouncing it off the floor, while your partner throws the ball up high. The final part of the exercise is to throw two balls simultaneously to your partner. This helps to combine your reflexes with improved eye-to-hand co-ordination.

Step 3
Stand 3m (10ft) from a wall, with your partner. The distance between you and your partner should be 2-3m (about 6½-10ft). Throw the ball against the wall so that it bounces towards your partner, who catches it and throws it back. Vary this exercise by throwing the ball with a bounce, so that it goes floor-wall-partner or wall-floor-partner.

Step 4
Place a container (such as a bucket) about 2m (6½ft) from the wall. With your partner, throw the ball into the bucket by bouncing it against the wall followed by the floor, or the floor then the wall.

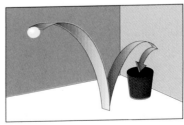

To make these exercises more fun, you can introduce an element of rivalry, such as by counting the number of misses. This will also help to improve your concentration.

SKILL

2 BACKHAND

*The backhand is one of the two most important strokes
used in table tennis, the other being the forehand*

THE BACKHAND is a less natural stroke than the forehand, as it incorporates a more limited range of movement, but it is easier to learn. Since your "feel" for the ball and co-ordination are still developing, we will begin by learning strokes in which the bat and playing hand remain within your field of vision at all times.

OBJECTIVE: To learn the backhand strokes. They can be used in either an aggressive or a defensive game. *Rating* from • to •••

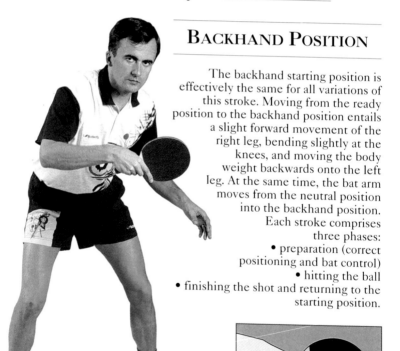

BACKHAND POSITION

The backhand starting position is effectively the same for all variations of this stroke. Moving from the ready position to the backhand position entails a slight forward movement of the right leg, bending slightly at the knees, and moving the body weight backwards onto the left leg. At the same time, the bat arm moves from the neutral position into the backhand position. Each stroke comprises three phases:
• preparation (correct positioning and bat control)
• hitting the ball
• finishing the shot and returning to the starting position.

Backhand grip

BACKHAND STROKES

The most typical strokes played, when the ball has bounced off the playing surface, are the **half-volley** (counter stroke) and the **push**. We will start by learning these two shots, as they are relatively straightforward. Remember to hit the ball gently at this stage. Hitting the ball too hard will make learning the stroke more difficult, and it will also increase the number of mistakes you make. You can increase the strength of the shot as your technique and proficiency improve. Try to keep the ball in play for as long as possible, hitting it at least ten times to your partner. When you wish to change the direction of the ball, and hit it in a straight line, turn your body, bat arm, and your feet slightly to the left.

Learn the elements of the backhand game by hitting the ball cross-court (diagonally) to your partner.

• **WRIST**
Remains firm at all times.

BALL •
Hit at its highest point.

BAT •
The face is kept open, in relation to the table.

FEET •
Lightly bent at the knee.

BACKHAND PUSH

This is one of the slowest backhand strokes. It is played with your knees slightly bent, and the right leg forwards. The ball is hit with a slightly open bat face. Shifting your body weight from the left to the right foot and keeping your knees bent at all times, try to hit the ball as it reaches its highest point after bouncing on your side of the table.

The wrist of the bat hand must remain firm, while the forearm gives the ball the right amount of speed and backspin. The backhand push is most commonly used in response to an opponent playing the same stroke. It is also used to return service. Since this stroke enables accurate returning, it is an ideal preparation for mounting an attack.

SKILL

2

BAT
Inclined by moving the wrist.

ARM
Almost fully stretched in the follow-through.

BAT
At right angles relative to the playing surface.

BACKHAND HALF-VOLLEY

This stroke is played with the legs and feet in the same position as for the backhand push. The bat should be kept approximately at right angles to the playing surface. However, at the moment of impact with the ball, the face of the bat should be changed to an acute angle, thereby "covering" the ball and increasing control of the stroke. The wrist movement must be accompanied by a forwards movement of the arm, until it is almost fully outstretched. The half-volley is typically used in response to an opponent's topspin shot.

BACKHAND DRIVE

This is the most dynamic and aggressive backhand stroke, and consequently one of the most rewarding to play. As this shot is difficult to master, a separate chapter has been devoted to it, which is scheduled for the second day of your weekend (see pp.54-57).

FOOTWORK AND POSITIONING

When playing aggressive strokes (half-volley, drive, or even a backhand push) remember not to move your right leg too far forwards. How far you move this leg forwards should also be determined by the tempo of the game: the quicker the tempo, the smaller the distance. Otherwise you may find that you do not have enough time to prepare or deliver a shot when changing to the forehand stance, which could easily result in an error. The precision of a backhand stroke is determined by the position of the elbow in relation to the bat.

Meanwhile, the position of your elbow is also determined by how far you move your right leg forwards. The greater the distance, the higher the position of the elbow should be, as this enables you to hit the ball harder.

For the half-volley and push strokes, the elbow should always be kept level with the bat.

BODY
Moving forwards.

BAT
Kept at an obtuse (open) angle relative to the playing surface.

LEGS
Knees bent, with the body weight resting on the right foot.

LEGS
Wide apart, and bent at the knees.

BACKHAND CHOP

This stroke is the defensive version of the backhand push, which it closely resembles, and is used to counter an aggressive shot from an opponent. Start by assuming a ready position about 1-2m (3-6.5ft) from the table, with your feet placed wide apart, knees bent, and the right leg slightly forwards. Just before returning the ball, move your body weight forwards and onto the right foot. At the same time, make a long sweeping move towards the ball with the bat arm. The face of the bat should be open, at approximately 180° (depending on the force of the spin). Make sure that your knees remain bent during this stroke. The backhand chop is used mainly by players favouring a defensive game. Its accuracy depends on correctly reading the type of spin that the opponent has applied to the ball.

3 FOREHAND

*The forehand stroke determines the character,
dynamics, and tempo of a game*

DAY 1

THE FOREHAND stroke confers various advantages that can easily
dictate the nature of a game. Moreover, a strong forehand combined
with good footwork enables a player to make aggressive shots from
virtually any angle. When following these exercises, use your
instinct to help develop your own "feel" for the ball.

OBJECTIVE: To learn the most natural stroke in table tennis.
Rating from • to •••

THE FOREHAND POSITION

Unlike the backhand
stroke, there is no single
starting position used to
play the forehand. The
majority of forehand strokes
are played with the left foot placed
forwards and the knees bent (as
illustrated). However, this position
does not apply to the half-volley and
the forehand push, which are played
with the right foot forwards.

Forehand grip

FOREHAND HALF-VOLLEY

Starting from the ready position, move your left foot slightly forwards (right foot for a left-handed player) and adjust your right foot slightly sideways, in relation to the base line of the table. At the same time, move the bat arm backwards from the neutral position. Shift your body weight from the right foot to the left, while also moving the arm towards the ball. The bat, which at the beginning of the swing is held at a 90° angle to the playing surface, should then be inclined so that it "covers" the ball on impact. The movement of the bat arm should follow a straight line, parallel to the playing surface. Meanwhile, the elbow should be held at the same level as the bat throughout the stroke. The forehand half-volley can be an effective response when an opponent has also used a forehand half-volley, or a topspin service.

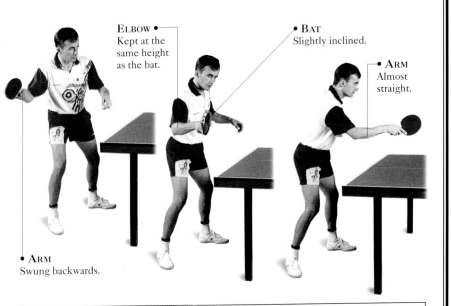

ELBOW
Kept at the same height as the bat.

BAT
Slightly inclined.

ARM
Almost straight.

ARM
Swung backwards.

TRAINING TIPS

Having played a stroke and hit the ball, return as quickly as possible to the ready position. The best way is with a **jumping action,** using both of your feet simultaneously. Doing this will provide you with valuable extra time before having to play the next shot. While training, try not to hit the ball low over the net. This will help you to recognize the type of spin that has been applied to the ball, and also to reduce the tempo of the game. In turn, this will make it easier for you to practise the strokes, and to maintain longer rallies with your partner.

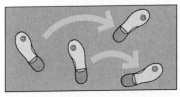

Returning to the ready position by "jumping"

SKILL

3

FOREHAND PUSH

The easiest of all the forehand strokes to play is the push. As with the half-volley, the ball is hit above the surface of the table. The push is one of two forehand strokes (along with the so-called forehand flick) that is played by moving the right foot slightly forwards, towards the oncoming ball. When changing from the ready position and moving the right foot forwards, simultaneously take the bat arm slightly back, and hold the bat with an open face. Additionally, while moving towards the ball you should be transferring your body weight onto the right foot. As you play the shot, continue to follow through by moving your arm up until it is fully outstretched.

ARM •
Held back.

• **BODY**
Inclined forwards.

BAT ARM •
Almost straight at this stage.

• **RIGHT FOOT**
Placed forwards.

——— THE INITIATIVE ———

The most important consideration when playing a match is to try and take the initiative from your opponent. Playing a variety of penetrating forehand strokes is an ideal way of achieving this.

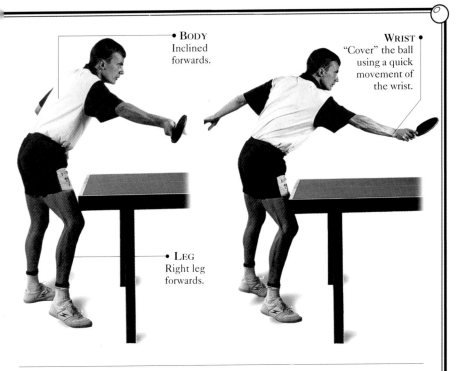

BODY
Inclined forwards.

WRIST
"Cover" the ball using a quick movement of the wrist.

LEG
Right leg forwards.

FOREHAND FLICK

The forehand flick is similar to the push, and is particularly effective against a short ball. The difference lies in the way in which the ball is hit. The face of the bat is kept open, while a swift movement of the forearm and wrist takes the bat up and over the ball. The flick is mainly used by advanced players to open up the game and take the initiative.

TRAINING

When training, keep repeating the forehand push and forehand flick, while also gradually increasing the force and pace of each shot. Practise your forehand by initially playing cross-court shots. When you want to practice hitting the ball in a straight line, change the position of your body and feet in relation to the end of the table (see illustration at right). Once you have learned to hit the ball in both directions, try to alternate hitting the ball cross-court with hitting it down the line. Make sure that you assume the correct position and adjust your footwork for both types of shot. Start training by playing push shots, then advance to playing more demanding **backhand** and **forehand** half-volleys.

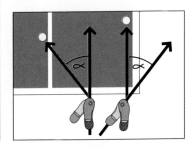

SKILL

3

• ARM
Swung far
back.

BAT •
Closed,
almost parallel
to the playing
surface.

ARM •
Completes the
movement to
its natural
conclusion.

• LEGS
Knees
bent.

LEGS •
Swiftly
straightened.

FOREHAND DRIVE

The forehand drive, like the
backhand, is one of the most
aggressive strokes, and mastering it
requires long training. This stroke
dominates modern table tennis and
we will therefore devote an entire
lesson to it, on day two of the
course (see pp.50-53).

A dynamic forehand
drive is one of the
most effective point-
winning strokes.

FOREHAND CHOP

This difficult stroke is essentially a defensive shot, delivered from the second or even the third zone, 2-3m (6½-10ft) from the table. It is used when the ball falls below the level of the playing surface. Standing with the left foot forwards, the angle of the bat face is determined by the type and degree of spin that has been applied to the oncoming ball. The bat arm is initially taken to hip or even knee level, in an extended movement that keeps the angle of the bat face in relation to the playing surface. The angle of the bat may also be changed, depending on your own skill and tactical play. You may wish to make the game even more difficult for an opponent (for example, by using a non-spin defence instead of a chop). The use of special rubber bat surfaces (such as those with long pimples) can create further difficulties for an opponent. Remember that even a small change in the bat angle can significantly alter the type of spin.

• LEFT FOOT Rests forwards.

• BAT Held at an open angle.

LEGS • Bent at the knees, making it easier to move your body weight.

The other two forehand strokes: blocking topspin balls and the forehand lob, will be covered later in the course (see p.58 and p.66).

SKILL

4

SERVICE

A successful service depends on a player's inventiveness and ingenuity

WHILE THE SERVICE IS USED TO START A GAME, it can also give the server an enormous advantage. The service is one of the most complex elements of the game, in view of the range and degree of **spins** that can be imparted to the ball. The choice of **spin**, as well as the strength and accuracy of the service, depend on how well you co-ordinate your body movement with the action of the bat arm. As the service can be played from both sides of the table, either a forehand or backhand service can be used. In theory (and this happens increasingly in the modern game), the service can win a point outright, by forcing an error from your opponent.

OBJECTIVE: Learning how to use the service to your best advantage.
Rating from • to •••

BAT POSITION •
The angle of the bat face is relative to the playing surface, usually between 90-120°. This allows for a stroke with minimum topspin.

SIMPLE BACKHAND SERVICE

Assume the ready position, in the middle of the left-hand side of the table. Hold the ball in one hand and the bat in the other, beyond the end of the table. Toss the ball about 30cm (12in) high, move the free arm to the left, and hit the ball as it descends.

GENERAL RULES

The ITTF regulations cover every element of the service action. The initial requirement is to toss the ball, by using the free hand, to a height of at least about 16cm (6in). Prior to the toss, the ball should rest freely in the palm of the hand, with the thumb held outstretched. The ball should be tossed in a direction that is defined as "close to vertical". While the ball is still in the air, and prior to.being hit, the bat must be held above the height of the playing surface. Additionally, the server must strike the ball beyond the end of the table, but also within the "line" that runs from the

Long service

server's hip to the shoulder of the bat arm. If any of these regulations are not followed, the server will lose a point. In a singles game, the service may be delivered in any direction into the opponent's side of the table. The ball is required to bounce first on the server's side of the table and then, having crossed the net, the ball must also bounce in the opponent's court. If the ball should hit the net and fail to cross over into the opponent's side of the table, or if the ball fails to bounce on the opponent's side of the table, the server will lose a point.When a properly served ball touches the net, but still bounces onto the opponent's half of the table,

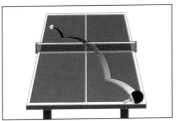

Short service

this is known as a "net" or a "let", and the service is repeated.
Although the service may be delivered in any direction to the opponent's side of the table when playing singles, when playing doubles the ball must be served diagonally from the right-hand side of the table. Additionally, the service must be played from behind the end of the table, just as in singles, otherwise the server will lose a point. Therefore, when serving you must pay close attention to the position of both the ball and your bat, in relation to the playing surface. The accuracy of the service, as well as the type of spin that is applied to the ball, both depend on careful co-ordination of the hands and body

Preparing to serve

movement, as well as your balance. The service can be divided into two principal types:
• short service – this term describes a stroke that positions the ball so "short" that it could bounce more than once on the opponent's side of the table;
• long service – this term describes a stroke that positions the ball so that it bounces only once on the opponent's side of the table, and then continues its trajectory beyond the playing surface.

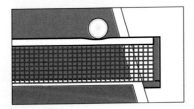

Net

SKILL

4 BACKHAND SERVICE WITH SIDESPIN

This dynamic stroke is a more complex version of the standard service. Instead of striking the ball with a forwards movement, the bat arm makes a rapid sweeping move across the body. As the ball descends, it is hit with the bat face held parallel to the end of the table. The angle of the bat is the same as for a standard service. If you have any problems, try moving the bat slightly forwards, prior to striking the ball; this reduces the spin but also ensures a safer delivery.

• **BAT**
Held at a 90-120° angle.

• **BODY**
The degree of "rotation" is relative to the strength of the stroke.

BACKHAND SERVICES WITH COMBINED SPIN

These strokes are a modified version of the service actions that apply sidespin. The difference lies in the angle of the bat at the moment of impact with the ball. In order to apply a combination of sidespin and backspin, you must remember to make the following changes from the standard service action, before making contact with the ball:
• the trajectory followed by the bat arm must be slightly curved in relation to the playing surface;
• the angle of the bat face must be changed from about 90° to a more open angle. It is the angle of the bat that, to a large extent, determines the degree of backspin. Applying a combination of topspin and sidespin to the ball is achieved in a similar manner. The only difference is that the angle of the bat, which is about 90° for a standard service, should be changed to an acute angle (up to around 60°), just before making contact with the ball. The trajectory of the arm curves slightly upwards, until the moment of contact with the ball. Once you have mastered the essential service techniques, you can develop your own approach, to create an innovative and individual service style.

FOREHAND SERVICE USING A SIDE GRIP

This service is frequently used in match play, as it enables the player to apply various types and degrees of spin to the ball, as well as varying speeds. This is the only stroke in table tennis where changing the grip is recommended, though only for the duration of the service action. Hold the bat so that the index finger rests sideways, along the backhand side. The thumb grips the bat on the forehand side, while the remaining fingers rest on the backhand side of the handle, and stabilize the grip. The hand that holds the ball should remain just beyond the end of the table. This may seem like an unnatural grip, but it allows for more effective use of the wrist, in order to impart both spin and greater speed to the

ball. In order to make this stroke as effective as possible, you must also have your elbow above the height of your palm. This position makes it easy for you to move the wrist in practically every direction, while also allowing you to impart any type of spin to the ball.

EYES •
By implying the direction of a service, you can influence your opponent's position.

BODY •
Assume the ready position, inclined at around a 60° angle, in relation to the end of the table.

BAT •
The angle at which you hold the bat in relation to the trajectory of the ball, combined with the appropriate movement of your wrist and forearm, enables you to impart any type of spin.

POSITION
Stand by the left-hand corner of the table, just beyond the sideline.

SKILL

4

POSITION
Assume the ready position, in the middle of the left-hand section of the table.

• PROJECTION
Place the ball on the palm of one hand, while holding the bat in the other hand, beyond the edge of the table. Project the ball vertically upwards, to a height of about 30cm (12in).

• ARMS
Move the free hand to the left. Its place will be taken by the bat arm, which strikes the ball on its descent, and directs it forwards.

ARM •
The bat arm is taken both upwards and backwards.

STROKE
Try to strike the ball with an open bat, about 20cm (8in) above the playing surface, swinging the bat arm towards the net. The angle of the bat relative to the playing surface should be between 90-120°.

BODY •
Swing the bat arm while "rotating" your body, which should also be leaning forwards, moving your body weight forwards and onto the right leg.

FINISHING THE STROKE •
Having struck the ball, complete the follow-through to its natural conclusion, then assume the ready position.

— TRAINING —

When practising your service, try to keep your arm and body relaxed, as tense muscles reduce the accuracy of your delivery. Try to perform a series of 10-20 identical serves, always aiming for the same spot on the opponent's side of the table.

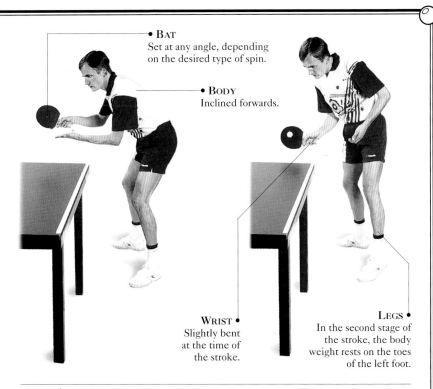

• BAT
Set at any angle, depending
on the desired type of spin.

• BODY
Inclined forwards.

WRIST •
Slightly bent
at the time of
the stroke.

LEGS •
In the second stage of
the stroke, the body
weight rests on the toes
of the left foot.

THE NATURAL (SHAKE-HANDS) GRIP SERVICE

This method of serving is now less popular. The movement and stroke combination are naturally limited by the body. The position assumed to deliver this type of service is the same as when using side grip, but the body is inclined slightly further forwards. Proceed as follows:
• project the ball upwards, while swinging the bat arm with the bat forwards;
• drop the free arm;
• strike the ball as it descends, with the hand movement directed towards you, and slightly forwards, bending the wrist at the moment of impact with the ball;
• continue to follow through until the movement reaches its own natural conclusion;
• return to the ready position.

Depending on the angle of the bat in relation to the ball's trajectory, the ball can be imparted with sidespin, topspin, or sidespin-topspin. The ball must be struck beyond the end of the table.

SKILL

5

SERVICE RETURN

DAY 1

Accurate service returns will hinder your opponent's effort to take the initiative

A WIDE RANGE OF SERVICE STROKES can be used to impart a variety of spins, which means that a practical and reliable response is essential. A good service depends less on force and more on precision, so when preparing to return service, try to concentrate on assessing the type of spin that has been imparted to the ball, and decide on the most appropriate response.

OBJECTIVE: Learning to return service as effectively as possible.
Rating from •• to •••

The main types of service return can be categorized as:
• defensive – typically used by defensive players, in the form of a push or a chop shot. This enables the server to take the initiative;
• aggressive – used by attacking players.
An accurate and decisive return of service will allow you to take the initiative and prevent an opponent from playing aggressively. The strokes most commonly used for this type of return are the topspin, half-volley, or smash.
The service return is the first stroke played directly into the opponent's court. The subsequent strokes are played in the same manner until the rally ends (until one player wins a point).
The principle of service return is to position the bat in order to counter the spin of the oncoming ball. Therefore the most important factors, apart from reading the spin correctly,

are the position of the body and the bat arm in relation to the ball, and the ability to move the wrist slightly, so that the stroke can be adapted, if necessary, to prevent an error. The correct way to prepare for returning the service is to assume the ready position. A right-handed player stands about 30cm (12in) from the table, to the left of the centre line; a left-handed player stands to the right.

A short service should be returned with
a flick; a long service with a drive or a
half-volley. Defensive players usually
return the service using a chop.
Whichever stroke you choose to return
a short service, you should position
yourself with the right leg forwards (or
the left leg forwards if you are left-
handed). At the moment of impact with
the ball, move the body weight onto
that leg. After playing the shot, push
against this leg in order to return to the
ready position. To return a long service
on the forehand side, assume a position
with the right leg placed slightly back,
and use this leg to return to the ready
position after you have played the ball.

When returning a long service on
the backhand, move your left foot
back slightly and use it to return to
the ready position, after playing the
stroke. Having learned the
backhand and forehand drives, use
this method to return a long service.
A strong and accurate topspin
response to a service is always the
most difficult one for an opponent
to return.

INSTANT DECISIONS

Having to return a short service that
bounces in the centre of the table will
force you to make an instant decision
about which side (backhand or
forehand) to use. By hesitating you will
lose valuable time, which is needed to
deliver an accurate return. Developing
your own instinct through practice and
match play will help you to make the
right decision.

An accurate return of service is a
crucial element to every game plan. An
accurate return enables you to take the
initiative away from your opponent.

SKILL

6

FOREHAND DRIVE

DAY 2

This aggressive stroke is also very useful for defensive players

TOPSPIN CAN BE IMPARTED to the ball in a variety of ways, depending on the zone in which the ball is hit. The forehand drive allows you to return the ball quickly and powerfully, regardless of the spin imparted to it by an opponent.

OBJECTIVE: To learn a stroke which can be used to mount an attack or to hit a winning shot. It is a difficult shot to play, but even more difficult to return. *Rating* •••

ARM
Straightening your bat arm, start the swing from a point above the right foot, co-ordinating the swing with your body movement. Keep the arm within your field of vision at all times.

EYES
Follow the movement of the ball.

BODY
Keep leaning forwards at all times. Start the stroke with your body sideways to the table and finish by standing with your face and body parallel to the table. Meanwhile, rotate your body according to the movement of the bat arm.

BAT
The angle of the bat in relation to the floor/playing surface should be about 60°. If at first you find it difficult to hit the ball, change the angle to about 90°.

LEGS
In the initial phase of this shot, bend your knees.

ARM
Initially almost straight, the arm is bent at the moment of contact with the ball.

FOOTWORK

Move your body weight forwards, from the right leg to the left, while also partially straightening both legs. This move in body weight should be accompanied by turning your feet towards the table. In this position you can play a powerful forehand drive. However, if you wish to play a more dynamic topspin stroke, you can – at the last moment – move the right leg forwards. As soon as you have finished playing the shot, you should return to the ready position by using a jumping action.

ARM
Try not to hold the left arm too near the body; holding it back and slightly bent will help you maintain balance during the stroke.

ARM
Contact with the ball is preceded by an accelerating movement of the forearm and wrist, which imparts greater spin.

FEET
At the moment of contact, you should be standing on the balls of your feet.

LEGS
Straighten them gradually.

TRAINING

Start practising the forehand topspin shot by "shadow" training. Stand in front of a large mirror, in which your entire body, including your feet, is clearly visible. Move your left foot forwards, then extend it slightly further forwards. Both your feet should be at a slightly odd angle in relation to the mirror (which represents the table).

Try to combine all the elements of this stroke, by working your legs, body, and bat arm simultaneously, following the suggested routine. Remember to keep leaning forwards at all times. Practise the forehand drive by hitting the ball diagonally across the table. Once you can hit a successful forehand drive, try to play a series of 5-7.

SKILL

6

BOUNCE OF THE BALL

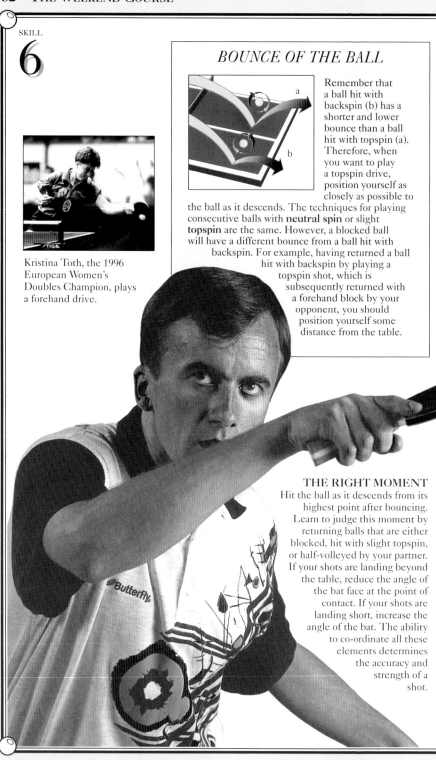

Remember that a ball hit with backspin (b) has a shorter and lower bounce than a ball hit with topspin (a). Therefore, when you want to play a topspin drive, position yourself as closely as possible to the ball as it descends. The techniques for playing consecutive balls with **neutral spin** or slight **topspin** are the same. However, a blocked ball will have a different bounce from a ball hit with backspin. For example, having returned a ball hit with backspin by playing a topspin shot, which is subsequently returned with a forehand block by your opponent, you should position yourself some distance from the table.

Kristina Toth, the 1996 European Women's Doubles Champion, plays a forehand drive.

THE RIGHT MOMENT

Hit the ball as it descends from its highest point after bouncing. Learn to judge this moment by returning balls that are either blocked, hit with slight topspin, or half-volleyed by your partner. If your shots are landing beyond the table, reduce the angle of the bat face at the point of contact. If your shots are landing short, increase the angle of the bat. The ability to co-ordinate all these elements determines the accuracy and strength of a shot.

POSITION
A topspin forehand drive is an excellent response to a chop shot. Position yourself as though you were placing your entire body under the ball.

DYNAMICS
A drive must be played in a dynamic manner, in order to reverse the **spin** imparted on the ball by an opponent.

TOPSPIN DRIVE
There are various types of topspin. The type shown here is played "from low to high"; others (for example, counter topspin) are played very flat (see p.85).

ARM
Do not shorten the movement! Reducing the extent of the movement will make it more difficult to learn this technique.

FOOTWORK

With your body weight resting on the right foot, move the left foot forwards while also straightening and slightly rotating your entire body. Make sure that you do not keep your leg muscles taut as you play consecutive drives – having completed each individual stroke, relax your leg muscles, perhaps by using a light upward or sideways jumping action.

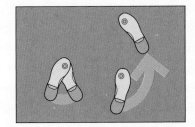

SKILL

7

BACKHAND DRIVE

This additional topspin shot offers a wide range of uses in the game

ALTHOUGH THE TOPSPIN BACKHAND is a less natural shot to play than the forehand, it is nevertheless easier to learn. The narrower range of movement made in front of the body also allows you to combine great accuracy with forceful **topspin**.

OBJECTIVE: To learn a stroke that is aggressive when played from the first zone; when played from other zones, the degree of spin forces an opponent to play a defensive reply. *Rating* •••

FINISHING THE STROKE
Having hit the ball, continue moving your arm upwards to its natural conclusion. At this stage your body weight should be moving onto the right foot.
Having completed the stroke, return to the ready position with a jumping action.

ELBOW •
On making contact with the ball, and immediately afterwards, the elbow of the bat arm should be at the same height as the ball.

ARM •
As your body weight moves forwards, steady your balance by using your free arm.

LEGS •
End the stroke standing on the toes of your left foot.

ELBOW
Initially, the elbow of the bat arm is above the bat hand.

LEGS
Bent at the knees.

BODY
Rotating your body slightly to the left, with the free arm held back, will help you to maintain your balance.

SWING
Move your right foot slightly forwards and further to the right.

ARM
Drop the free arm to the height of the left hip.

STROKE
Straighten your body and both legs, and move your bat arm upwards and slightly forwards. Strike the ball about halfway through the arm movement, with a rapid movement of your forearm.

CORRECTING ERRORS

Use a large mirror that, with the benefit of imagination, takes the place of the table, and will help you to detect any errors in your positioning and footwork. This part of the learning process should be done as "shadow" training, without using a bat or ball. Try to imitate the movements illustrated. Stand with your feet apart, legs bent at the knees, and your body leaning slightly forwards. The bat arm and the free arm should both be above the level of the table, and slightly bent at the elbows.

SKILL
7

• **SWING**
Notice how low you must drop
the bat in order to attack the
ball with a fast-moving bat.

• **HAND**
Initially slightly "dropped", the wrist
remains slack, so that it can be used to
generate accelerated hand movement
just before hitting the ball.

• **STROKE**
At the point of contact,
increase the strength of the
stroke using your wrist,
and by straightening your
legs and body.

COMPLETING THE SHOT •
In the final stage of the shot,
you should almost straighten
your body.

FOREARM •
The basis of this
stroke is the
forearm movement.
Notice the changes
in the positions of
the hand and elbow.

FOOTWORK

If an opponent returns your **topspin** shot in a way that
forces you to change position, you should try moving
towards the ball by using a
jumping action. This will
prevent you altering your
balance and ensure4s you
will be ready for the next
shot. In order to play more
aggressively, the left foot
may also follow through at
the end of a dynamic shot,
by moving towards the right
foot (see diagram).

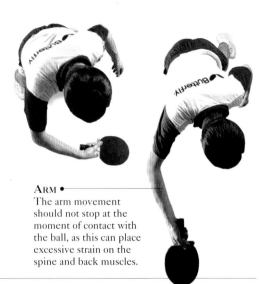

SWING
The same move viewed from above shows how the position of the body changes, following the movement of the arms and legs.

ARM •
The arm movement should not stop at the moment of contact with the ball, as this can place excessive strain on the spine and back muscles.

TRAINING

After practising numerous "shadow" strokes, repeat the exercise using a bat. The angle of the bat in relation to the playing surface should remain between 60-80°. The degree of spin imparted to the ball, and the pace of the shot, depend on co-ordinating each element of the stroke, including wrist movement. A relaxed, comfortable grip enables you to make dynamic movements with your wrist, and to project the ball with topspin by hitting over it. Practise playing topspin backhand shots across court, returning balls that are hit without any spin or slight topspin. Once you can hit individual topspin backhands, try playing a rally in which you hit 5-7 consecutive topspin backhands. Having built up consistency, try playing a series of topspin backhands with your partner,

applying various types of spin to the ball. First return a chopped ball, with the remaining shots being blocked and returned either flat or with slight topspin. Remember that to play the first backhand you have to move forwards and get "under" the ball. The remaining shots should be played from a certain distance, which is enforced by the change of spin. Try hitting deep into your opponent's court, as this is difficult to return and generally results in a defensive response.

Zoran Primorac of Croatia, the 1993 World Cup winner, scores an important point by playing a backhand drive.

SKILL

DAY 2

8 BLOCKING TOPSPIN BALLS

The block is the simplest and most typical method of returning topspin balls

A TOPSPIN SHOT can be returned in various ways, for instance by using a defensive **chop** played from the second (defensive) zone, a **topspin counterattack**, or even a smash – when the topspin brings the ball up high. However, the simplest shot is a block, which is also a defensive method of returning topspin shots. The accuracy of a blocked shot relies on reading the spin, as well as good positioning at the table.

OBJECTIVE: To learn a simple defence against topspin strokes.
Rating ••

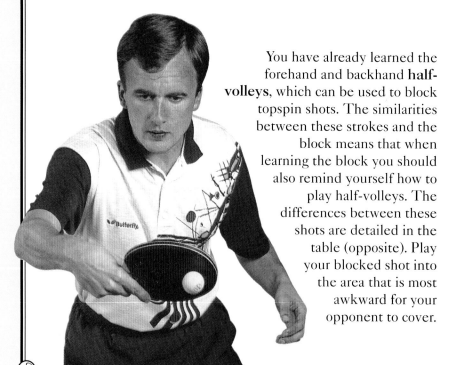

You have already learned the forehand and backhand **half-volleys**, which can be used to block topspin shots. The similarities between these strokes and the block means that when learning the block you should also remind yourself how to play half-volleys. The differences between these shots are detailed in the table (opposite). Play your blocked shot into the area that is most awkward for your opponent to cover.

HALF-VOLLEY	BLOCK
FEET For a forehand stroke, the left foot should be placed slightly forwards; for a backhand stroke the right foot should be forwards.	**FEET** Parallel to the edge of the table, for both forehand and backhand strokes.
BODY For a forehand stroke, assume the ready position, turning slightly to the right; for a backhand stroke, turn slightly to the left.	**BODY** Perpendicular to the ball's trajectory, for the entire duration of the stroke.
ARM Make a wide, sweeping movement when playing either a backhand or forehand.	**ARM** A short movement made just in front of the body.
BAT Open at all times, the angle should be slightly less than 90°.	**BAT** "Close" the bat at the moment of contact with the ball, reducing the angle up to 45°, depending on the spin.

THE BLOCK

Replying to a topspin shot by playing a block is, by definition, a defensive move. However, playing an accurate block can force an opponent to play a defensive reply, and enable you to take the initiative. Good concentration will help you to "read" the spin imparted to the ball, and position the bat at the appropriate angle. When playing the block, try to relax your wrist and forearm muscles. Taut muscles increase the probability of errors. As a ball hit with topspin tends to accelerate rapidly after bouncing on the table, try to block the ball immediately after it has bounced.

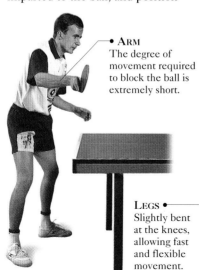

• **ARM**
The degree of movement required to block the ball is extremely short.

LEGS •
Slightly bent at the knees, allowing fast and flexible movement.

• **BAT**
Slightly "close" the bat face, in order to block a ball hit with heavy topspin.

9 THE WINNING SMASH

Properly executed, this shot should win you the point

THE ABILITY TO HIT AGGRESSIVE and accurate shots depends on several factors. These include the ability to read the **spin** imparted to a higher ball, and also to position your body correctly. Forcing an opponent to play a higher, more defensive shot usually takes three or four strokes, and even then a high-bouncing ball will not necessarily result in an outright winner – which means that consistency is crucial.

OBJECTIVE: To learn how to finish a rally by winning the point.
Rating from •• to •••

FOREHAND SMASH

You must be in the right position before attempting to play a smash. Starting in the ready position, move your body weight forwards to the balls of your feet, which will enable you to move into position quickly. Using the forehand is the most dynamic and effective method of executing a smash.

SWING
Without taking your eyes off the ball, move your right arm up and back.

STANCE
Turn the left side of your body towards the oncoming ball. The ball's trajectory should be in line with your right shoulder.

• **BAT**
The bat is in the "open" position.

• **ARM**
This should move down as you turn your body.

FEET •
Use a quick jump to move your feet apart, with the left foot forwards.

ATTACK
Co-ordinating your arm and body movements, hit the ball close to its highest point, after it has bounced on your side of the table.

• **BAT**
This should remain "open" throughout the entire movement.

BODY •
A stroke is not limited to the arm movement. It must be accompanied by a co-ordinated movement of the entire body.

BODY •
This should be almost straight; move your body weight from the right foot to the left foot.

LEGS •
Don't limit movement with your right hip; the right leg should "follow" the ball. Move your body weight forwards onto the left foot, and turn the left foot towards the left.

SKILL

9

BACKHAND SMASH

The backhand smash is used far less than the forehand, and is played principally when a high ball bounces deep in the backhand court. If you do not have enough time to run around the ball and play a forehands smash, get into position for a backhand by placing the right foot forwards and lifting the bat arm. Holding your elbow above the bat will enable you to move your forearm and strike the ball with a downward movement. If you have to play this stroke in the course of a rally, only use it once, continuing (if necessary) with a forehand smash, which is much easier to execute.

USEFUL TIPS

During the initial stages of learning the game, do not hit the ball too hard. Instead, concentrate on learning the correct technique for each stroke. Only increase the pace of the stroke gradually.

When preparing to play a smash, observe your opponent's position carefully, and aim the ball at the spot from where it will be most difficult for your opponent to return it.

If you have to smash a chopped high ball against a defensive player, remember that this requires you to move forwards and be positioned "deeper" under the ball. Also, the bounce from a chopped ball is much shorter compared to a ball with little or no spin. In this instance, the path of the bat arm when playing the stroke is almost parallel to the playing surface. Do not hit the ball while standing with your body upright and your legs straight. Straightening the body blocks the movement of the hip, knees, and tarsal joints. Moreover, playing the shot incorrectly can also lead to injury. Having completed the shot, move back into the starting position. If you are faced with a **short lob**, move nearer the table. For a **long lob,** move backwards quickly by using a jumping action, as this type of ball is far more difficult to play.

SWING •
The bat arm is
taken far back.

Ding Yi of China playing in Austria.
His game is based on an excellent
forehand smash (penhold grip).

STROKE
As with the forehand
smash, strike the ball
when it reaches its
highest point.

• FEET
The centre of
gravity rests on
the left foot.

ARM •
Bring the move
to its natural
conclusion, to
prevent excessive
stress being put
on the spine.

• FEET
At the moment of contact,
the body weight shifts to
the right foot.

10

DEFENSIVE LOBBING

DAY 2

This effective return could save you a seemingly lost point

IN TABLE TENNIS it is possible to come out on top in practically any situation, if you have good defensive strokes. One of the most effective elements is an accurate defensive lob. This shot may not only prolong your opponent's attempt to win a point, but also give you the opportunity to prepare your own counter-attack. While the defensive lob is sometimes played entirely from necessity, it can also be a positive, tactical element of a defensive game.

OBJECTIVE: To reinforce a defensive game with a new stroke. *Rating* ••

The lob can be played from either the **backhand** or **forehand** side. The most important consideration is your position in relation to the table and the ball. Always try to position yourself at the centre of the area from which you could play the ball, assess the strength of your opponent's stroke, and adjust your position (distance from the table) accordingly.

STANCE
There is no classic stance for playing the lob; you should adjust yourself according to each individual situation.

LEGS
To play the lob, the legs are often bent at the knees, as when playing a drive, particularly when you have to reach for a low ball.

A Defensive Backhand Lob

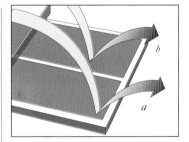

POSITION

Stand in the ready position, about 2-3m (6½-10ft) from the table, within the "backhand" zone marked by the extension of the left sideline and the centre line of the table. Straighten your body and bat arm, holding your arm at chest level. The face of the bat, held in the backhand position, should be "open". Concentrate on the ball and remember that the speed of the ball will depend on the strength of your stroke. However, the lob is one of the few shots in the game that does not generally allow enough time for you to assume the proper stance.

STROKE

Try to return the ball with a high, "arched" trajectory, mainly through the movement of your hand. Bending your bat arm, and using an almost mechanical movement upwards until the moment of contact with the ball (as it descends), should direct the ball upwards. Follow through until the arm is almost straight. If you find this hard, "open" the bat face, and keep it at an obtuse angle in relation to the playing surface.

TRAINING

When you first start to practise this shot, ask your partner not to smash the ball too hard, as less aggressive shots will help you to develop a feel for the pace, spin, and trajectory of the ball.
After about an hour of practising the **backhand** lob, when you feel that you have mastered the basic shot, start aiming your returns deeper into the opponent's court, and then try to apply a slight topspin to your lobs as well. A deep topspin lob is by far the most difficult shot for an opponent to smash, while also forcing your opponent to move away from the table.

Try aiming the lob deeper into your opponent's court (a). A short lob (b) provides an opportunity for a winning smash.

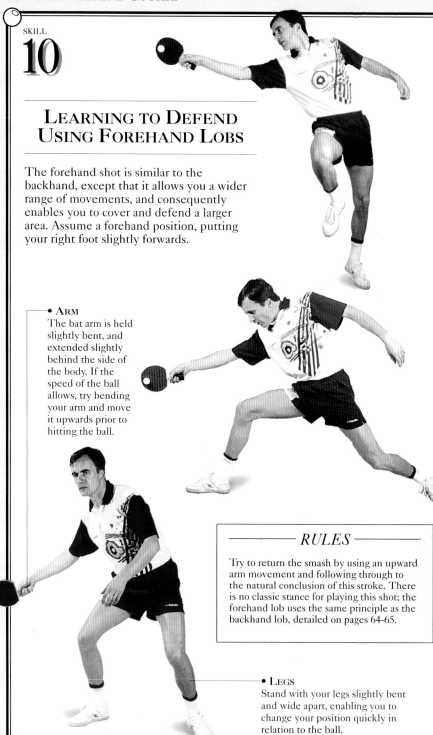

SKILL

10

LEARNING TO DEFEND USING FOREHAND LOBS

The forehand shot is similar to the backhand, except that it allows you a wider range of movements, and consequently enables you to cover and defend a larger area. Assume a forehand position, putting your right foot slightly forwards.

• ARM
The bat arm is held slightly bent, and extended slightly behind the side of the body. If the speed of the ball allows, try bending your arm and move it upwards prior to hitting the ball.

— *RULES* —

Try to return the smash by using an upward arm movement and following through to the natural conclusion of this stroke. There is no classic stance for playing this shot; the forehand lob uses the same principle as the backhand lob, detailed on pages 64-65.

• LEGS
Stand with your legs slightly bent and wide apart, enabling you to change your position quickly in relation to the ball.

BODY BALANCE
As the rally unfolds, you will sometimes
be forced to play a shot having lost your
balance; in this case you should use your
trunk to balance your body.

HIT
Impart **topspin** to the ball by using
your wrist at the point of contact. Aim
the ball deep into your opponent's
court, as near as possible to the end
line of the table.

Having learned to play both types of lobs, ask your partner
to deliver smashes in both directions. When
combining backhand and forehand returns,
remember to hold your bat in the neutral
position after each shot.
Move forwards quickly to meet the ball;
after returning it, take a step back without
taking your eyes off the ball. In between
shots, keep your leg muscles loose, for
example, by using a slight jump. This
also makes it easier to position yourself
for the next shot. If the lob you play
is too short, your opponent may also
play a short ball; you should approach
it with your right leg forwards
(right-handed players) and play a
backhand or forehand return.

FEET
If you have to run to play a short ball,
do it by using a side-step, which is the
most economical way to move for most
table tennis strokes.

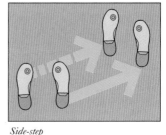

Side-step

SKILL

11 ELEMENTS OF DEFENSIVE PLAY

DAY 2

A review of the shots and methods used in a defensive game

A GOOD DEFENDER displays great patience and ingenuity in playing the ball. Having already practised defensive shots on previous pages, we will now see how they can be combined within a defensive game. Today's defenders are very quick, supremely fit, and have the patience of a saint. They concentrate continually on trying to force an opponent into committing an error.

OBJECTIVE: To recap the main defensive strokes. *Rating* from • to ••

TACTICS

When you have learned to recognize different types of spin and are able to play various strokes, think about the tactical side of the game. Success often depends on being able to surprise your opponent. Your choice of bat is also an important factor when playing a defensive game. The blade should allow for a high degree of control, together with a slow speed of return. The handle should be straight, allowing you to change sides easily (with the bat featuring different rubbers on each side, for example, smooth and pimpled), helping you to make play more difficult for your opponent.

STROKES PLAYED WITHIN THE FIRST ZONE

Lisa Bellinger-Lomas, 1992 European Runner-up. This outstanding defender is seen here playing a brilliant forehand chop.

PUSH
This is the most common stroke for returning the service or a short ball. Aim to exploit your opponent's weak spots.

FLICK
Although rarely used by defensive players, this shot can add a vital element of surprise, particularly when different rubbers are used on each side of the bat.

SERVICE
The most important elements of the service are height and length. Play a service that enables you to return to zones 2-3, (that is, a semi-long or long service), because these are the most secure zones for a defensive game. For variety you should also include some short services and aggressive strokes.

Kouji Matsushita, 1995 Japanese Singles Champion, playing a dynamic chop defence.

FOREHAND CHOP
This shot is detailed in the chapter on forehand shots. It is usually played as a defensive shot within the second and third zones. In the first zone it can be used to return a short service. It is usually played in response to a topspin drive or a forehand smash.

11

STROKES WITHIN OTHER ZONES

THE BACKHAND CHOP (as illustrated here) is detailed in the chapter dealing with backhand strokes. The defensive version of this shot is usually played within zones 2-3, from a low position with the knees bent and the right foot forwards (for right-handed players). This stroke is frequently used in response to a drive or smash, though it can also be used to return a long service.

SMASH
Try to play a smash when an opponent feeds you a high ball; a defensive player must also be aggressive, as surprise is an important element of the game.

FLOAT
This stroke is frequently used by defensive players. Hitting the ball with an "open" bat, as a substitute for a backhand or forehand chop, also changes the rhythm of a game.

FOREHAND COUNTER-TOPSPIN
This is a defensive reply to topspin, typically played from the second zone, though also more aggressively from the first zone (see p.85).

— MAKING IT DIFFICULT FOR THE OPPONENT —

By applying chop to the ball, and playing it as deep as possible into your opponent's court (see right), you will make it difficult for an opponent to reply. This approach will also give you more time in which to play the right return. As a defensive player, make use of the different types of rubber surface on each side of the bat. Applying a different type of spin to the ball, or an aggressive, deep **service**, will change the pace of the game, and create further difficulties for your opponent.

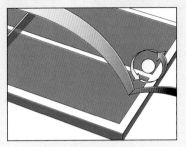

DEFENSIVE LOB
This shot is usually played as a last resort. Increasingly, classic defensive players use a combination of defensive and aggressive shots. This is largely due to the players using a combination of rubber surfaces, resulting in one side of the bat being suitable for defensive play and the other for an aggressive game.

FOREHAND CHOP
(as illustrated)
This is one of the defensive player's favourite strokes. It is played not only from the first zone, but also from other zones, when its function is similar to that of the corresponding backhand shot.

12 DEVELOPING TACTICS AND MATCH PLAY

Having learned the technical elements of the game, it is time to try them in action

AFTER ACQUIRING the basic skills of table tennis, you have to practise combining them within a game. This will enable you to see how successfully you can play the shots you have been working on. In table tennis you win points either by forcing an opponent to make an error, or by playing an aggressive game. The following set of exercises will help you to launch an attack following your own service, or to assert your own game when returning an opponent's service. The exercises should also enable you to assess your strengths and weaknesses so that you can focus on the area of your game that needs the most work.

FOLLOWING UP ON YOUR OWN SERVICE

• If you decide to play a topspin or side-topspin ball, you should be prepared for your oppponent to play an aggressive return. Move slightly back from the table and

raise the bat; then play the most aggressive half-volley or topspin shot that you can. If the service is then returned with a push shot, it will be far easier for you to attack the ball.

• If you decide to play a backspin or side-backspin service, then the reply you should expect depends on the length of the service.
In reply to a short service, expect a push shot, to which you should respond with topspin (see illustration at left).
In reply to a deep service, an opponent may use topspin, which you should return with a block; whereas you should reply to a push shot with topspin.

FOLLOWING UP ON YOUR OPPONENT'S SERVICE

• The appropriate response to a service that is hit short, with no spin or topspin, is a flick or half-volley. Having played your return, move quickly to the ready position, a short distance from the end line of the table, and be ready for your opponent to attack.

• A short service hit with backspin or side-backspin should be returned with a push shot. Play it short, if you can, which will provoke your opponent to attack this difficult ball (see illustration below). If you play a

Yoo Nam Kyu, Olympic Champion in Seoul (1988). This left-handed Korean is a master of the forehand drive finish.

long return, you can expect a topspin ball from your opponent, which you should return with a block.

• A long service should be attacked with topspin, regardless of where the ball bounces. This will give you a chance to take the initiative – use it! Try to develop your own tactics, using a variety of strokes, and use these in matchplay. Try to anticipate an opponent's returns as the rally unfolds – anticipation is vitally important in this sport.

Chen Xinhua (representing England), several times medal winner at the World Championships, is a defensive player who is also comfortable playing an aggressive game.

AFTER THE WEEKEND

Develop your technique by practising both alone and with a partner

HAVING LEARNED THE BASICS, it will of course take more than a weekend to perfect your game. Joining a club, and playing various opponents, is an ideal way of achieving this.

RULES AND REGULATIONS

Learning the principles and regulations of the game

•

BEFORE YOU START playing matches, familiarize yourself with the rules and regulations. Toss a coin to decide which player chooses whether to serve or return, or which side of the table to start playing from. If a player chooses to serve, the opponent can choose the side of the table from which to receive the service.

RULES

A point begins with a service delivered by one of the players. In the course of a game, service alternates between both players, with each player having five consecutive services. The point is won when an opponent is unable to return the ball correctly. A match can be played over the best of either three or five games. A game is won when a player has scored 21 points, with a lead of at least two points. If the score is levelled at 20:20, play continues until one player gains a two point lead, which wins the game. The break allowed between games is 2 minutes. If the match goes into a final game (either the third or the fifth game), players change sides when one player has reached 10 points.

The service is the only stroke where the ball must first bounce in the server's court, and after crossing the net, bounce in the opponent's court. Subsequent strokes are played by hitting the ball so that it bounces only in the opponent's court. If the service bounces in the opponent's court having touched the net, the service must be repeated.

THE TWELVE-STROKE SYSTEM

This system comes into effect when a game has lasted for more than 15 minutes, but without either of the players having reached 19 points. Players take it in turn to hit one service each, and attempt to win a point within twelve consecutive strokes (not counting the service). Otherwise, the player who hits a legitimate thirteenth consecutive stroke automatically wins the point. In 1995, the rules governing a player who returns a ball that is hit "out" were changed. Returning a ball that has not bounced in your court, and which is played beyond the boundaries of your court, does not result in the loss of a point. You only lose a point by returning a ball that has not bounced in your court, if you play it within the boundaries of your court.

REGULATIONS

SERVICE
• Before being tossed for the service, the ball must be stationary within the centre of the palm (which is held open). This hand must remain beyond the end line of the table, and above the level of the playing surface.

• The ball is tossed vertically, to a height of at least 16cm (about 6in), and hit as it descends from the toss. The ball must bounce first in the server's court, cross the net, and then bounce in the opponent's court. In doubles, it must first bounce in the server's right-hand court, before bouncing in the receiver's right-hand court.

• Before serving, the bat arm must be held above the level of the playing surface.

• The ball must be hit behind the end line of the table, but not beyond the "line" linking the server's leg, hip, and shoulder (adjacent to the serving arm).

GAME
A player wins the point whenever an opponent:
– makes an error serving
– hits the ball into the net

– makes an error when returning an opponent's service
   – hits the ball beyond the boundary of the opponent's court without it bouncing on the playing surface
   – fails to hit the ball
   – hits the ball twice in succession within a single shot
   – touches the net with the bat or any part of the body
   – touches the playing surface with the free hand
   – moves the table during a rally
   – hits the ball with a part of the bat which is forbidden, or with any part of the body
– fails to win a point, whenever the "twelve-stroke" system has been employed
– points are also lost in doubles if the ball is played out of sequence.

DOUBLES

A successful doubles pair often combines two different styles of play

A DOUBLES PAIR needs to establish a close understanding of each other's style of play, so that both players can make the most of their individual skills, while also developing their sense of teamwork. In doubles, the tactical approach is more important than the power of a shot, so co-operate fully with your partner, rather than trying to dominate a rally individually.

"LEFT-RIGHT" POSITIONING

An ideal doubles pairing is one that combines a left-handed player with a right-handed partner. This allows for optimum positioning at the table, while also promoting forehand play, which enables a greater pace of shot and more aggressive play. Another advantage of this combination of players lies in using the left-handed player to return the service. As the ball must always be served into the right-hand court, a left-handed player can assume a position that is closer to the ball, enabling greater accuracy and pace in the service return. Both of the players should position themselves close to the table, in the same way they would for a singles game.

REGULATIONS GOVERNING DOUBLES

There are two important differences between the regulations that govern the singles and the doubles game. In doubles you win a point whenever:
• an opponent's service bounces outside the opponent's right-hand court, or outside the receiver's right-hand court (as illustrated in the bottom right-hand corner)
• either of the opposing players hits the ball twice in succession. In doubles, players in each pairing must hit the ball alternately.

RULES OF THE DOUBLES GAME

Just as in a singles game, a coin is tossed to see which pair is given the choice of whether to serve or to receive service, or indeed, to choose which side of the table to begin the game. Having taken their places at opposite ends of the table, the service is hit cross-court from the right-hand side of the table. This part of the table is delineated by the 3-mm line that extends along the centre of the table to the end line, dividing the table into two halves. When serving, the ball must first bounce within the server's right-hand court, before crossing the net and bouncing in the right-hand side of the opponent's court. The return of service, as well as any subsequent strokes, may be hit into any part of the opponent's court, although partners must hit the ball alternately. The scoring system in doubles is the same as that used in singles. If a match goes into a final game (either the third or fifth game), the players change ends when either pair reaches 10 points. The order of service remains unchanged, with the receiving pair alternating when returning service.

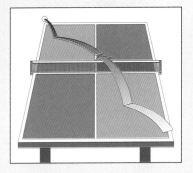

THE "RIGHT-RIGHT" AND "LEFT-LEFT" POSITIONS

When a doubles pair comprises two right-handed players, they can adopt various positions to return an opponent's service:

• A partner stands behind the returning player's right shoulder. Having returned the ball, a player moves to the left, allowing space for a partner. When using this approach, the distance between players must be sufficient to allow unrestricted shot-making.

• The partner of the returning player stands behind the returning player's back. After hitting the return, a player moves to the right, allowing the partner sufficient space to get into position for the next stroke.

A doubles pair comprising left-handed players can only position themselves as follows:

• The partner should stand at the right-hand corner of the table, behind the left arm of the returning player. After the return has been hit, the player moves to the right, creating sufficient space for the partner to assume the most advantageous position at the table.

MIXED DOUBLES

The same principles for positioning at the table apply when playing mixed doubles. This is played at a competitive level alongside men's doubles and women's doubles. Doubles matches (including mixed doubles) are usually played over the best of three games, whereas men's and women's singles are usually played over the best of five games.

A mixed doubles pairing using the "right-right" position. Notice the difference in the players' positions compared to the "left-right" system (as shown on p.79).

SERVICE IN A DOUBLES GAME

The author has achieved numerous successes in doubles. Here he is accompanied by his long-time partner, Leszek Kucharski, after winning the Bronze medal at the 1987 World Championships in Delhi.

The type of return you are able to play does of course also depend on the nature of the service. The type and degree of spin that is applied to the service, as well as the length and height, plays a crucial role in a doubles game. A short and low service, which is played close to the net, is a typical tactic used by aggressive teams. This prevents their opponents from launching an attack with their service return, while also enabling the servers to assume the initiative. Defensive pairs frequently use a light-long service, with the intention of provoking an error from their opponents in the service return.

SERVICE RETURN

A short and accurate return of service may enable your team to go on the attack, and thus take the initiative away from your opponents. An aggressive, accurate smash or a precise flick shot can have a similar effect on your opponents.

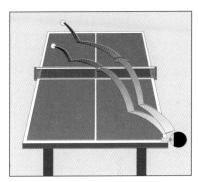

Various types of service

DOUBLES TACTICS

When playing consecutive shots with your partner, follow the rule of positioning yourself at the centre of the table (see p.82), assuming that this is relevant to the position of your partner, and in relation to the ball. Do not attempt to play risky shots too often – concentrate instead on playing with your partner as a team. Communicate with your partner throughout a match, which will help to develop your understanding of each other's game. For instance, before serving, use your free hand to signal to your partner, under the table, what type of spin you intend to apply to the ball; this will help your partner to prepare for the opponent's return.
Try to match the **pace of your game** to that of your partner, and concentrate on consistency. Hitting the ball with an irregular rhythm will increase the chances of an error.

TACTICS IN SINGLES MATCHES

When players are of an equal standard, tactics often determine who wins

PLAYING A MATCH is a measure of various technical skills, and of a player's ability to combine these skills effectively. Your game will also be influenced by how an opponent plays. Remember that there are no perfect players: everyone has weaknesses. You must try to identify these, which should become more apparent as the match progresses. Developing either an aggressive or defensive strategy to exploit your opponent's weaknesses should force errors and win you points.

THE TACTICAL IMPORTANCE OF THE SERVICE

An accurate, strategically placed service can give you the initiative, and enable you to impose your game-plan on an opponent. Similarly, a short, accurate service can set you up to mount an attack on an opponent. However, an opponent may also be able to attack a short service, which could place you in a defensive position. If you decide to play a long service, remember that a service that bounces as close as possible to the end line of the table is generally the most difficult for an opponent to return effectively.

It is also vital to maintain an element of surprise, by varying the length and direction of your service, and also by applying a variety of spins to the ball – which should keep your opponent guessing.

THE "CENTRE" RULE

Having played a shot, always try to position yourself in the middle of the table, so that you can cover shots to either side of the table with equal speed and efficiency. Moreover, try to play consecutive shots in a direction that ensures the subsequent "centre" of the table is relative to your current position.

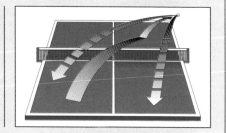

PLAY ZONES

This term is used to describe a player's distance from the end line of the table, at the point of contact with the ball. The first zone, known as "play at the table", refers to a distance of 1m (about 3ft) from the end of the table. Subsequent zones also refer to a player's distance from the end of the table, with the second zone referring to a distance of 2m (about 6½ft), while the third zone is 3m (about 9½ft). Aggressive players should position themselves to hit the ball within zones 1 or 2, whereas defensive players are usually more comfortable within zones 2-3. If you have to leave your preferred zone during the course of a rally, try and return to it as quickly as possible; the shots that you play from your prime zone are your most dangerous weapon!

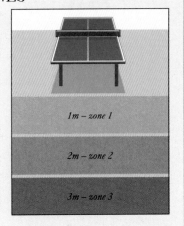

1m – zone 1

2m – zone 2

3m – zone 3

POSITION AT THE TABLE

Your own instinct and experience, combined with practice, will confirm on which side (either backhand or forehand) you play your most accurate and confident shots. Consequently, you can adapt

the standard position at the table to capitalize on your strengths. For instance, if your forehand is a particular strength, you may be able to make more effective use of this shot by standing deeper in the backhand corner, or by changing the emphasis of the game towards your forehand. However, adapting your position in this way will entail having to move faster, and will also mean altering the pace of your game, for instance by changing from a quick, half-volley game to using topspin. Players who prefer a backhand game should stand nearer to the centre of the table, which will enable them to play backhand strokes more frequently and more effectively. During a rally, try to direct your returns as close as possible to the end line of the opponent's court. This will make it more difficult for an opponent to make accurate returns, while lengthening the trajectory of the ball will also give you more time to get into position.

SHOTS FOR ADVANCED PLAYERS

Learning strokes that require special skills

•

TABLE TENNIS is a fascinating game, and you will probably want to learn some of the more complex elements. The weekend course covers the basic strokes, to which you can add more advanced techniques. The forehand and backhand **counter-spin** and the **stop-block**, for instance, are technically difficult strokes, and require a well-developed "feel" for the ball. Needless to say, learning to play table tennis entails far more than one weekend!

BACKHAND COUNTER-TOPSPIN

This a specific type of topspin, played in reply to the same stroke delivered by your opponent. It differs from the classic topspin drive by the almost parallel positioning of the feet in relation to the end line of the table, and by a more acute angle of the bat, which "closes" over the ball at the point of contact. You can make this stroke more dynamic with a jumping action using your left leg.

POSITION
In zones 1-2, your legs should be wide apart with knees bent and the right foot forwards.

BAT •
A more acute bat angle is used if the ball is hit above the playing surface, rather than beyond it.

• LEGS
The left foot can move forwards in the final stage of a shot hit from beyond the table – then resume the ready position.

BENDING YOUR KNEES

Both the forehand and backhand counter-topspin shots will not be dynamic or accurate enough, unless your legs are apart and your knees are bent when playing the shot. In addition, when using topspin shots, you must remember to use your wrist. An effective wrist action will generate a greater pace, while also imparting a greater degree of spin to the ball.

STANCE
Assume the forehand position: legs wide apart and bent at the knees, with the left foot forwards. Move your body weight to the front part of the foot.

HIT •
Try to hit the ball as it rises, "closing" the bat at the point of contact.

• **LEGS**
In the final stage of the stroke, the right foot can be moved quickly forwards. Then return to the ready position with a jump.

• **LEGS**
Move your body weight to the right foot; use this foot to push yourself forwards and to the left.

FOREHAND COUNTER-TOPSPIN

Although returning a topspin shot using topspin is difficult, it can be any effective reply. The technique is similar to that for "regular" topspin, but it must be dynamic enough to counter the topspin already applied and "replace" it with your own spin. The bat arm moves less steeply than in a regular topspin shot (the nearer to the table, the "flatter" the movement should be), while the bat angle is also closed at the point of contact. To help achieve this shot you can reinforce the hand movement by "pushing" with your right foot.

FOREHAND COUNTER-TOPSPIN STRUCK OFF THE BOUNCE

Another type of forehand counter-topspin is applied to balls hit above the playing surface. This entails striking the ball as it rises from the bounce, or as it reaches the highest point after bouncing. It is the most dynamic of all topspin shots, played with the arm moving almost parallel to the playing surface. The angle of the bat is also relative to the trajectory of the bat arm.

STOP-BLOCK

When an opponent plays a topspin or **half-volley** shot from zones 2-3, an effective return is the stop-block. This shot takes the pace off the ball, and frequently catches opponents out of position. The accuracy of a stop-block depends on your position at the table, and being able to read the spin and trajectory of the oncoming ball. There are two types of stop-block. One applies sidespin to the ball, while the second involves moving the bat arm slightly back at the moment of contact with the ball.

POSITION
Stand by the table with your legs almost parallel to the end line of the table.

BODY •
Leaning slightly forwards.

FOREARM •
Held parallel to the playing surface.

BAT ARM •
Moves back to cushion the impact of the ball, and guides it to fall gently over the net.

STOP-BLOCK WITH SIDESPIN

Another version of the stop-block is played by moving the bat arm in a 90° plane across the table, in relation to the oncoming ball. This will reduce the trajectory of the ball, while also imparting sidespin. The backhand stop-block is illustrated on this page.

ARM
Moves parallel to the end line of the table.

BODY
Leaning forwards for the duration of the stroke. The arm movement is followed by a strong "rotation" of the body.

LEGS
Slightly bent, and positioned parallel to the end of the table.

BAT
Held near the body, in an "open" position throughout the entire movement of the stroke.

SIMILARITIES

Does the technique of playing the stop-block remind you of any other shots? The backhand stop-block is actually the reverse of the backhand service, while the forehand stop-block is the reverse of the forehand flick. Mastering the technique of simple strokes also helps you to learn more difficult shots.

FINAL COMMENTS

Some helpful tips

FOR SOME PEOPLE, TABLE TENNIS is simply a game that is played for pleasure, while for others it is a way of life or even a profession. However, novices and professionals can experience similar problems with health and concentration. This chapter will help you to avoid at least some of these potential problems.

POSITIVE MENTAL ATTITUDE

Table tennis is an intense game: the speed of the ball combined with the numerous types of spin that can be used, makes it vital that a player concentrates and remains focused the entire time. Consequently, a player's rate and quality of progress, as well as match-playing ability, largely depend on having a positive mental attitude. Playing as many matches as possible is the best way of developing this attitude. You must also learn how to deal with stress and pre-match nerves, which are a problem for experienced players as well as amateurs. Vigorous warm-up exercises before the match, chatting to someone, or even listening to a personal stereo can all help. Finding the most effective way of dealing with stress may even require months of effort, but it is certainly worth trying. Developing a positive mental attitude will not only enable you to learn the game faster, but you will also find it easier to deal with stress, which means you will gain far more pleasure from the game. Once you become more confident

and believe in yourself as a player, you will also improve your power of concentration. A momentary loss of concentration, even if you already have a strong lead over an opponent, can prove to be significant. On the other hand, try not to dwell on losing a point. Instead, concentrate on winning the next point, and try to identify your opponent's weaknesses. In the final game of a match, play the shots that won you points earlier. Try also to impose your own style of play on an opponent, or to use tactics which prevent opponents from utilizing their strengths. By following this advice, you can be sure that it will be your opponent who is stressed – and not you!

PREVENTING INJURIES

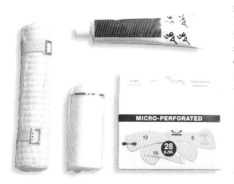

As with all forms of physical exercise, table tennis can cause various injuries and ailments. You should be aware of the most common injuries, as well as the preventive steps that you can take in order to avoid injury.

The most common areas in which injuries are sustained include:
• neck and back. These injuries occur almost exclusively in more advanced and more experienced players, as a result of prolonged pressure on the spine, caused by years of training;
• tarsal joints – the pressure on these joints stems from the rapid speed of movement that is necessary at the table;
• knee joints – bending the knees is an important element of playing numerous shots;
• shoulder, and joints within the bat arm – caused by the dynamic movements required to play numerous shots.

In order to prevent these injuries from occurring, you should end every training session by performing a set of stretching exercises, as recommended in this book. You should also maintain a regular exercise and fitness routine. Remember that a weak body is more prone to injuries than a supple, fit body. At least 10 per cent of the total time you spend playing table tennis should be devoted to fitness training!

Other health problems can result from smaller injuries sustained during training, such as pulled muscles and tendons, or sprained joints. However, these injuries often arise from an inadequate (or even a non-existent!) warm-up routine. Remember that every training session or sparring game should start with at least 15 minutes of general warm-up exercises, including:
• gentle jogging
• stretching and twisting routines
• rotating your trunk and arms
• gentle stretching exercises for your arms and legs
• jumping up and down on the spot, as well as from side to side

Remember: prevention is better than cure.

Petr Korbel, the outstanding Czech player, whose favourite approach features topspin shots on both wings.

A FEW WORDS OF ADVICE

Adam Giersz, Chairman of the Polish Table Tennis Association and former coach of the Polish National Team, pictured giving the author of this book advice during a break between games.

• You cannot have too much general fitness training – every form of exercise will develop some group of muscles. Particularly recommended are team games (such as soccer and basketball), which increase hand-and-eye co-ordination, and sports such as tennis and swimming, which improve general mobility.
• Take advantage of your natural assets and build your training routines around them. If one side of your body is stronger (the backhand side or the forehand) it is easier to decide on your approach in a close match.
• Hide your nervousness, to gain a psychological advantage over your opponent. This principle should be applied from the very first moment you take the bat in your hand.
• The trend among professionals in the 1990s is towards shorter movements, greater dynamics. Shortening your moves, especially in the follow-through, gives extra time to prepare for the next shot.
• More dynamic strokes mean that players now try to play from as near to the table as possible. Players who position themselves further back in the defensive zones have a much lower chance of winning a point. If you want to be successful, play from within the first zone.

Always play fair and remember: in sport you can win friends, but you can also lose them.

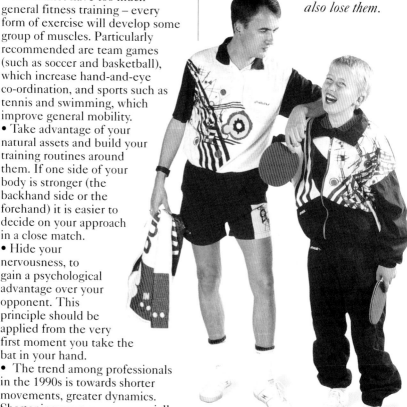

MATCH PLAY AND COMPETITIONS

Practising individual strokes can become repetitive and boring, so you should vary your training routine by incorporating match play. Try to allocate fixed days and times for this, and play with a variety of partners. Make arrangements to play with your friends as well, because this will help you to stick to a regular training routine. You can book a table at your local club or sports hall. If you can buy your own table, and play in a large room or garage, so much the better. You do not have to take the professional regulations on space around the table too seriously, though you should remember that too small a space will make it more difficult to learn.

Tournament successes may bring you impressive trophies. Here is a selection of Andrzej Grubba's collection.

Taking part in competitions will also give you extra motivation to train. Ask for information at your local sports centre or Table Tennis Association about competitions for players of your own standard. Entering competitions is also a great way to meet people with similar interests to yours. I wrote at the beginning of this book that playing table tennis, even at a purely amateur level, can become a great adventure. Taking part in competitions is an ideal way to begin this adventure.

Csila Batorfi, of Hungary, plays a dynamic backhand drive.

GLOSSARY

B

- **Backhand** – a stroke delivered from the left-hand side of the body (by right-handed players), with the back of the hand facing the direction of the stroke.
- **Backhand diagonal** – the area on the left side of the table, at both ends of the table (for right-handed players).
- **Back-step** – a quick and effective method of moving backwards, to position yourself in defensive zones.
- **Best of five** – a match won when one side has three games.
- **Best of three** – a match won when either side has two games.
- **Blade** – the wooden part of the bat, made of several layers of plywood (usually 5-7).

C

- **Centre line** – the thin, continuous line, 3mm (about ⅛in) wide, joining the midpoints of the end lines and marking the service areas for doubles games.
- **Chop** – a stroke that imparts backspin to the ball, often delivered from a defensive play zone.
- **Counter-topspin** – a stroke that imparts the ball with topspin, played in response to the same stroke played by an opponent.

D

- **Drive** – a stroke that imparts the ball with heavy topspin; it can be delivered from the backhand or forehand side.

F

- **Flick** – striking a short ball with an open bat, using a swift forward hand movement.
- **Forehand** – a stroke delivered from the right-hand side of the body (by right-handed players), with the palm of the hand facing the direction of the stroke.
- **Forehand diagonal** – the play area to the right of the court, on both halves of the table (for right-handed players).

H

- **Half-volley** – hitting the ball with an open bat off the bounce (either above the playing surface or in zone 1); delivered either from the backhand or forehand side.

J

- **Jump** – the basic method of changing position in preparation for the next stroke; generally used to cover distances of 1-2m (about 3-6½ft).

L

• **Lob** – a stroke played from a defensive zone, preceded by a natural sweeping movement; sometimes used by defensive players to change the pace of the game.
• **Long lob** – a high return from a defensive zone, into the opponent's court, close to the end line.
• **Long service** – a service in which the ball, having bounced on the opponent's court, bounces outside the opponent's court.

N

• **Neutral position** – the bat is held in a way that allows the fastest response to play a backhand or forehand. The bat is almost perpendicular to the end line of the table and playing surface.

O

• **Open bat** – bat held at almost 90° over the playing surface. Typically used to play a half-volley and smash.

P

• **Pace of the game** – the speed at which the game is played.
• **Penhold grip** – otherwise known as the "oriental" grip for holding the bat. The handle is held between the thumb and the index finger that marks the forehand side – the only side used with this type of grip; the remaining fingers support the reverse side of the bat, stabilizing the grip.
• **Playing the first** – playing the ball from the opponent's service or from the return of the player's own service.
• **Push** – hitting the ball off the bounce (over the playing surface); which is suitable for imparting the ball with backspin.

R

• **Reaction time** – the speed of reaction to the opponent's stroke, incorporating reflex and anticipation.
• **Robot** – a ball-throwing device, which offers various spins, directions, and frequencies, creating an excellent substitute for the conditions encountered in match play.
• **Rollaway** – a type of playing table; it has wheels and, after being folded up, can easily be moved and requires very little storage space.

S

• **Service** – the first stroke that begins the rally for each point. The ball is played from behind the end line of the table; it must initially bounce on the server's side and, after crossing the net, bounce on the opponent's side.
• **Shake-hands grip** – otherwise known as the "European" method of holding the bat, allowing the player to hit the ball with both sides of the bat. The handle is held with the index finger pointing forwards, marking the backhand side. The thumb and the remaining fingers grip the handle, meeting on the other (forehand) side.
• **Short ball** – a short return of a long ball that is played by an opponent.
• **Short lob** – a high return of the ball that lands close to the net, usually played from a defensive zone.
• **Short service** – a service that crosses the net and bounces on the opponent's court, without leaving the opponent's court.
• **Sidespin** – a type of stroke that imparts the ball with side rotation. It is most commonly applied in combination with topspin or backspin.
• **Side-step** – the most efficient way of moving within zones 2-3, parallel to the end line of the table.
• **Spin** – rotation of the ball around its own axis while in motion. The different types include: topspin, backspin and combined spin (side-topspin and side-backspin).
• **Stop-block** – the method of block-returning (close to the net) a topspin ball played from a defensive zone; this alters the character of the spin and an opponent's rhythm.

INDEX

B

backhand 32-35
backhand position 32
backhand stroke
 block 58
 chop 35, 70
 counter-topspin 84
 drive 34, 54-57
 float 70
 half-volley 34, 59
 lob 65
 push 33
 sidespin 27, 86
 smash 62-63, 70
 stop-block 86
ball 12
ball-throwing machine
 (robot) 17
bat 8, 10
bat cover 12
blades
 all-round 10
 fast 10
 slow 10
body balance 67
brush (for bat surface) 13

C

catapult effect 11
catching the ball 31
centre rule 82
cleaning sponge 13
clothing 14-15
competitions 91
concentration 24, 88
cross-court shots
 backhand 33
 forehand 39

D

doubles game
 mixed 80
 positions 79-80
 rules 79
 service 81
 tactics 81

E

edging tape 13
equipment
 additional 13
errors
 correcting 55
European grip
 see shake-hands grip
exercises
 shaping up 18-19
 speed 19
 stamina 19
 stretching 20
 with the ball 31
 with the bat 30

F

fitness 9
flick 39
footwear 9, 14-15
footwork
 in backhand play 56
 in forehand play 53
 jumps 37, 56
 side-step 67
forehand 36, 41
forehand stroke
 block 59
 chop 41, 69, 71
 counter-topspin 85
 drive 40, 50-53
 flick 39
 float 70
 half-volley 37, 59
 lob 66-67
 push 38
 sidespin 27
 smash 60-61, 70
 stop-block 86
 topspin see drive

G

grip 10
 forehand 36
 penhold 22
 service side grip 45

shake-hands 23
side grip 45-46

H

handle see grip
hitting the ball 52

I

initiative 38
injuries 89

L

lob 64-65, 71

N

natural grip service see
 shake-hands grip service
net 43

O

oriental grip see penhold
 grip
overlays see rubbers

P

point game
 best of five 76
 best of three 79
 competitions 91
 rules 76
position
 at the table 25, 83
positive mental
 attitude 88

R

ready position 24-25
robot 17
rubber adhesive 12
rubbers
 dimpled 11
 pimpled 11
 special 11
rules of
 doubles game 79
 playing space 16-17

point scoring 76-77
service 77
running 19

─────── *S* ───────

service
  combined spin
    backhand 44
  forehand with side
    grip 45-46
  long 43, 81
  return 48-49
  shake-hands grip
    service 47
  sidespin backhand 44
  simple backhand 42
  short 43, 81
shirt 14
shorts 14

socks 14
spin
  backspin 27
  combination 27
  sidespin 27
  topspin 27
sponge 13
spray for
  degreasing rubbers 13

─────── *T* ───────

table
  construction 16-17
  dimensions 16
  markings 16
  play zones 83
  rollaway 17
  tactics and match play
    72,73, 82

tennis bag 15
track suit 15
trainer *see* ball-
  throwing machine
twelve-stroke system 76

─────── *W* ───────

warm-up exercises 89

Andrzej Grubba played for Poland between 1976-1996, competed in three Olympic Games – 1988, 1992, 1996 – and was runner-up in the 1996 European Doubles Championships. His greatest sporting achievements include:
– winning the World Cup (1988, Wuhan, China)
– winning Europe TOP-12 (1985, Barcelona)
– winning 15 medals at the World and European Championships
– voted "Sportsman of the Year" in 1984 by readers of the Polish sports publication *Przegląd Sportowy*
– co-founder of the CTTP (Club of Table Tennis Professionals)

The publisher wishes to thank *Tamasu Butterfly Comp. (Tokyo)* for the loan of, and permission to use, photographs of current top players; and Dr. Adam Giersz, who acted as a consultant for this book.